Negotiation Mastery

Tools for the 21st Century Negotiator

Simon Horton

First edition published in 2012

© Copyright 2012

Simon Horton

Paperback ISBN 9781780922560

ePub ISBN 9781780922577

PDF ISBN 9781780922584

Published in the UK by MX Publishing

335 Princess Park Manor, Royal Drive, London, N11 3GX

www.mxpublishing.co.uk

Cover design by

www.staunch.com

Contents

FOREWORD

In the end, we all die. That is non-negotiable. Everything else, though, is up for grabs.

This book will *not* help you get a better deal with Death; save your energy, no one wins an argument with Death.

But most other things, we can help. Money, anybody? Sex? Negotiation is *the very stuff* of sex and money! Global domination? Trust me, you will have to do a lot of negotiating.

Maybe your plans are a little more everyday. Need to resolve that dispute with the noisy neighbour? Want to ask your boss if you could leave early? Guess what, that's negotiation.

Or do you simply want to bring about a world-wide shift in thinking to save the human race from imminent self-destruction and make the planet, at last, a safe and happy place for everyone?

It is all about negotiation.

Who is the book for?

So, yes, this book is for people involved in negotiations in a professional context but it is for anyone involved in negotiations – *and that means all of us.*

Want your partner to take the rubbish out? Want to move house? Want a promotion? How about getting 20% off the price of those boots? Or dealing with the taxman over your arrears? Want a record deal for your first album? Or your tenth? This book will help.

The plain fact of the matter is that anything that involves other people will at some point involve negotiation.

I have taught Negotiation Skills for ten years now. I have taught hostage negotiators, Magic Circle law firms, investment banks and the purchasing departments for some of the largest manufacturing companies in the world. Countless people have already benefitted from the material in this book and my aim in making it more widely available is to help more people get better results in their negotiations of whatever kind.

I do not pretend it will turn you into a negotiator – you are one already. That is a bit like saying it will turn you into a human being.

But I do hope it will make you a better one. Negotiator, that is. And hopefully a better human being, too, because whether it is the big stuff or the little stuff, negotiation really is the stuff of life.

And the better you become at negotiation, the better you will become at your life.

About the book

The book is *highly* practical. It will de-mystify negotiation, give you a structure and a process to follow. In a clear, "How to...", bullet-pointed format, you will learn everything you will need to get the best deal you can and close it in such a way you can sleep peacefully knowing it will be implemented fully as agreed.

You will learn how to deal with complex, dynamic, multi-party situations, how to deal with deadlock, how to defend yourself against strong-arm tactics, how to get your way when all the power is stacked against you.

It will give you techniques and tactics – right down to the level of 'If they say x, you say y'. But it aims to go beyond that too. It will give you advanced techniques, beyond the normal negotiation literature. It draws upon the fields of psychology, of body language, of economics, of neuro-economics, of game theory, of systems theory, of decision theory. It uses cutting-edge research to really give you that advantage in the negotiation.

Enjoy the journey

And enjoy the journey. On the way, you are going to read about classic negotiations from business, politics and the world of international diplomacy.

And you will also come across evil dolphins, famous urinals, starving artists and anarchist rock bands, the discovery of Viagra, the negotiating tactics of Genghis Khan, the informational value of horse manure, sausage duels, how to set up your own cult and words of wisdom from Val Doonican's mum.

Sound good? Ready to rock and roll? Let us start by defining some terms.

CHAPTER 1: INTRODUCTION

What is negotiation?

Negotiation is not actually very important. Nor is the agreement that follows, nor the contract, nor the signatures. All quite unimportant.

So, then, why write a book on it?

To answer this, let us first define our terms: what exactly is negotiation? Now, there are probably as many definitions of the word as there are negotiators but a good working definition might read something like:

"The process through which two or more parties come to an agreement on an action to be carried out"

Uncontroversial. And yet it makes explicit a critical fact that is often overlooked: that a negotiation is part of a bigger process. In fact, it is the first stage of the bigger process which unfolds as:

1. Negotiate
2. Reach agreement
3. Implement action

and of these stages, the most important is the last one, *by far*.

The negotiation counts for nothing, indeed the signed contract counts for nothing, if *what is eventually implemented* in the real world does not suit you; that proud piece of paper merely a receipt for deceit.

This is really quite significant. When we think of negotiating, we tend to think of the haggle, the cut-and-thrust, the arm-wrestle. But all of that is only the means to the end, there simply to facilitate the action that is to be implemented. All of the great victories you achieve at the bargaining table, all of the fine words with signatures next to them, will mean nothing if events ultimately follow in a different manner to how you would like.

This small detail, hidden away within the folds of a definition, has immense ramifications for how you should negotiate and much of the rest of the book will follow from it.

Here, before we run too far ahead of ourselves, let us highlight just one consequence: that the negotiated solution must be win-win in nature.

This is true even for selfish reasons. Even if I am the most ungenerous person, thinking only of my own profit, I should target a mutually beneficial result because if the other party is not satisfied with the agreement, they will not implement it. Or they will sabotage it or undermine it or implement it to the letter but not in the spirit. Conversely, if it is to their advantage as well as mine, they will put all their full energies behind it in order to make it happen.

Put starkly like that, it is a no-brainer.

This is our starting point. And if you ever question "Why win-win?", return to this page and re-read the definition.

What is mastery?

Negotiation is a skill and it is an art. That it is a skill means it can be deconstructed and learnt. And the way to learn a skill, a complex skill like negotiation, is to break it down into its sub-skills and then practise each of them.

That it is an art, however, means there is no prescribed approach that will produce the right result in all situations. Situations can be so complex and dynamic, indeed, people can be so complex and dynamic that you can apply one technique in one context and be successful and, the next time, apply completely the opposite technique and still be successful.

It is not "what" but "how". There is no golden rule for which tactic to use in which situation. Instead, it comes down to gut-feel.

This book will show you how to develop that gut-feel and become a master negotiator.

The artist learns the techniques and the rules but then throws them away to create something new and more beautiful. The jazz musician learns his instrument and his scales to perfection, but then consciously forgets them and relies on improvisation to create his music.

This is how you develop gut-feel: learn the strategies, the techniques, the tactics and the rules; apply them in days, months and years of conscious, attentive experience; and then forget them in order to create something more powerful.

This is the artistry of negotiation.

This is negotiation mastery.

Styles of negotiation

Broadly, there are two main styles of negotiation: win-lose and win-win.

The win-lose approach is where you try to get as much as you can from the bargain, even (or sometimes especially) at the other's expense. Win-win, on the other hand, does not believe that your gain has to be at the other's expense. Indeed, it believes that all parties gain *more* from working together than they would on their own; such are the benefits from sharing resources and collaborating.

A common belief is that win-lose strategies get better results than win-win. Another common belief is that the win-win approach is good in theory but, in practice, the other party is likely to play a win-lose strategy and win-win simply plays into their hands..

We will see that neither of these fears are grounded. We will see that win-win approaches will get you a better result than win-lose and that win-win does not imply allowing yourself to be walked over.

The beginner's conundrum – be nice or tough?

When I run a Negotiations Skills course, especially at Introduction level, delegates are often suffering from a dilemma regarding their attitude to negotiations. Put simply, should they be tough or should they be nice? Part of them wants to be nice to the other person because that is their nature and their mother told them to be kind to people.

But then they worry that if they are too nice the other person will walk all over them and rip them off, so they decide to be tough. After all, their father always told them to stand up for themselves. But *then* they worry that will mean *they* are being a bastard and they start to get confused.

This is the conundrum. In fact, it is not only relevant to beginners, many experienced negotiators have the same dilemma but they just put it to the back of their mind.

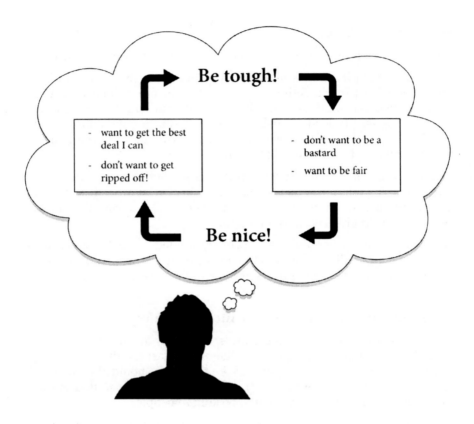

Fortunately, there is an answer.

The win-win dividend

Roger Fisher is one of the grandees in the world of negotiation. Co-author of the classic text "Getting to Yes", he is also Professor emeritus of Law at Harvard Law School and Director of the Harvard Negotiation Project.

He recounts how he often introduces his students to the "Arm Game", where he asks them to sit in pairs opposite each other across a desk, with their elbows on the desk and each holding the other by one hand. The rules of the game are that each player gets one point when the other person touches the desk with the back of their hand. The aim is to get as many points for themselves as possible in 30 seconds, without worrying about how many the other player scores.

When he says "Go", the students invariably launch straight into a determined arm-*wrestle* and the net result is perhaps a few points scored, two tired arms and the occasional sprained elbow.

Afterwards, Fisher demonstrates his own approach with a volunteer. When the 30 seconds starts, he surprises the volunteer by pulling their hand towards his side so that *his own* hand hits the desk, giving the volunteer a point. Whilst the volunteer is still surprised, Fisher pushes their hand back to other side of the desk and he now gets a point. Quickly, the student cottons on and they spend the rest of the 30 seconds, working together, alternating whose hand hits the desk.

The net result this way? A *far* higher number of points scored by both parties and no tired arms or injuries. This is the win-win dividend.

This is a perfect metaphor for negotiation. If you enter a deal with a win-lose approach, you will invoke a win-lose approach from the other party. Even normally reasonable people often get tougher in response to tough tactics. They dig their heels in and get more stubborn or become aggressive in return. Just like the arm-wrestle, all of the energies are destructive, cancelling each other out.

Alternatively, if you start with a win-win approach, they will respond in kind here, too. This is the arm-game. More points all round, no tired arms or injuries.

Win-win thinking is clever

Interestingly, nearly all the books and all the lecturers on negotiation agree on the win-win approach. Even those books that like to grab a bigger market by appearing tough and having Rambo-esque titles, they actually still end up in the win-win camp.

This is because, there is no getting away from it, win-win *does* get you your best deal.

I will start by unapologetically taking the higher ground. Wars, poverty, climate change, broken societies, broken families, hungry children – all come from win-lose thinking rather than win-win. What kind of a world do you want to live in? What kind of a world do you want your children to live in? One with wars, poverty, broken societies and broken families?

It's not clever.

But let us bring it a little closer to home. The emotions that evolve from win-lose thinking are anger, bitterness, hatred, fear, insecurity, unhappiness and similar. If you go in with a win-lose approach, these are the emotions that you will engender in the people around you. Do you really want to fill your world with these people around you?

The majority of our negotiations are actually conducted outside of work and it is extremely unlikely that you will be able to change your negotiating pattern from one context to another. Think about it: toughness and a blank face may be very effective in business but it will be crap in your family! If you conduct a win-lose approach at work, you will inevitably conduct the same approach in your personal life. And that, to be frank, is a recipe for a very unhappy life with few, if any, friends or loved ones and your children will be afraid of you.

I say, again, it's not clever.

And even if all of that falls on deaf ears let us bring it back to the deal: quite simply, win-win will get you the better deal.

We saw on the very first page that win-lose deals simply will not get implemented (at least, not in the way you would like) and we saw later that they often end up in stand-offs where no one gets a deal.

On the other hand, in a win-win deal the other party is incentivised to make it work and they will bring all their energies to making it happen: they will return your favours with favours for you, they will provide you with useful information, they will bring you useful contacts, they will point out things of benefit for you that you were not aware of and they will do things for you that you cannot do yourself.

You will create extra value by tapping into the wondrous fact of human interaction that one plus one can equal three. So everyone is happier, including yourself. In fact, especially yourself.

Win-win thinking *is* clever.

How to make 20 million enemies

Even for the most selfish of reasons, win-win is the best approach. With win-lose, the other person will try to stop you; with win-win, they will try to *help* you. Maybe I am missing something here but it does not seem too hard a choice.

I worked with one client many years ago who had previously been extremely successful but they were now going on a downward spiral. They probably had 20 million customers at the time but were losing them rapidly.

It became clear that the reason why they were losing their customer-base was because they were effectively playing a win-lose game with them. Without going into details, and thereby giving away the name of the company, their customer strategy was repeatedly and obviously at the customers' expense. It was win-lose – meaning *they had 20 million people fighting against them*!

Well, you are not going to win against 20 million people!

How about if they had a win-win approach: then they would have 20 million people fighting *for* them. Hmm, let's ask Einstein about that one.

When you look at some of the really successful products in recent times (for example, Google search, Facebook and the iPhone) this is exactly what you have – millions of customers who loved it so much that they praised it to the hilt to everyone they met and so becoming salesmen for that product.

Win-win is not *lose*-win!

There is an argument that since win-win has become the predominant view in business negotiation, there are sharks about who will take advantage of this.

Now, my view is that the fear of sharks is often overblown. According to figures from the U.S. Consumer Product Safety Commission report (1997), you are twenty times more likely to be involved in an accident with a room deodoriser or an air freshener than you are to suffer an injury from a shark attack. Watch out for those air fresheners!

However, joking aside, there is a fair point to be made. It is fair to say that, in going for win-win, if you are too nice-nice, the other party may take advantage of you.

So we are not asking you to be a charity (unless you are a charity, I suppose) and you should be on your guard against this.

Let us be clear: we are not advocating *lose*-win.

Nobody is saying be nice and roll over just so the other party likes you. It does not matter whether they like you or not, the important thing is that you get the best deal. And the best way to get the best deal is to go win-win.

Skilful negotiators are tough negotiators. They do not get bullied, they do not give in when they come across a problem.

But they are not aggressive or deceptive or play win-lose because they have found that ultimately this simply does not produce as good a result as the win-win approach. It is important to distinguish between strong and macho – strong is smart, macho is dumb.

Win-win, the Genghis Khan way

There are people who think win-win negotiating is for wimps. I have met people who even think negotiating *at all* is for wimps. After all, Genghis Khan never negotiated, did he?

Well, actually he did – and he usually offered a win-win solution.

Contrary to his popular reputation, Genghis Khan was a force for civilisation. In building an empire that was to stretch from Korea to Vienna, he introduced a legal code, a standardised script, a mail system, religious freedom, cultural tolerance,

---

a (largely) meritocratic government, free commerce and a generally better living standard.

Clearly, he could have better PR.

Ok, I admit, he did some pretty bad things too. He could be brutal and he ordered many massacres. But remember, this was the 12ᵗʰ century and massacres was what they did in those days.

It was rarely his first choice, though. On the contrary, he would offer cities and states the chance to join him peacefully and those that did *gained* in culture and prosperity from doing so. It was a genuine win-win solution.

Of course, if they did not take this option, he would gladly do win-lose – and he would do it very well. Nobody won an arm-wrestle with Genghis Khan.

(Footnote: We will not be advocating massacre as a specific negotiation tactic).

The Strong Win-Win approach

To be doubly safe regarding this concern, we will argue in this book for a policy of "Strong Win-Win". What is the difference between this and a traditional win-win approach? There are two differences.

Firstly, it recognises that win-win only works *if the other party plays win-win too*. So it places an emphasis on bringing out the win-win nature in the other person. Many people are naturally win-win, a few are resolutely not. The large majority waver somewhere in between. We will see many methods that can gently nudge or, if necessary, forcibly shove your counterparty towards win-win thinking.

Secondly, it stresses the importance of credibility and strength in the deal. Strong Win-Win will not be bullied, it will not be manipulated. It is a tough approach: it is tough on bullies, it is tough on stand-offs, it is tough on resolving complicated and challenging issues. And it also works with and alongside the other party to make sure that you both score the win-win dividend.

Interestingly, there is a positive circle involved here. Bullies will only bully those they know they can. If they know they cannot push you around, they are not going to try. So your strength, in itself, is a way to make them play win-win. And you can be more generous, yourself, if you feel secure that you will not be taken advantage of – if you cover your back, you will be more confident going forward.

This is the answer to the beginner's conundrum: get your best deal by using the Strong Win-Win approach.

The rest of the book will tell you exactly how to do this. However, before we go there, let us make one more distinction: between positional and interest-based bargaining.

Positional Bargaining

"For you, my friend, I give you special price of 200 Dirham".

It is the haggle. You are in the market in Morocco and you ask the price of an interesting vase you have seen. You wince at the price.

"For you, my friend, I *pay* special price of 40 Dirham".

He breathes in sharply and says, "175".

You smile, "Look, I'm not on a coach tour. Give me the Moroccan price, 60 Dirham."

"Here, sit down, I bring you some mint tea. You are a good person, I like you, I give you the Moroccan price, 140 Dirham."

You have a friendly chat, sipping fresh mint tea, with the smell and sounds of the bazaar in the background. You have a long conversation about the world and about football and eventually you get up to leave, "My last price, 80 Dirham."

"Ah, I will not make a profit on 80, let us agree on 120," and he shakes your hand.

"Ok, 90 and it's a deal".

He looks pained, "110."

You pick up your bag and start to walk out of the shop.

He says "100?"

"Deal!"

This scene illustrates what is known as positional bargaining, where you are fixed on your position and try to give as little ground as possible. In this example, the opening positions were 200 Dirham and 40 Dirham respectively and there was give and take until you both met at 100.

On a multi-dimensional deal, there may be several positions that are under discussion at once. For example, if you are looking to lease a fleet of cars for your company, you may have opening positions in mind for price, fuel efficiency, insurance, running costs, guarantee, number of cars, length of contract and many other variables. The negotiation is likely to involve give and take for each individually as well as for the whole package.

It can be like this example. It can be friendly, it can be an enjoyable process and you can reach an agreement where both parties are happy. If the shopkeeper makes a profit and you get an exotic vase at half the price you would pay back home, both parties have gained.

It can be like this, but not always. In fact, more often than not, focussing on fixed positions means that one party will win at the other party's expense. Any Dirham you save will be a Dirham lost by the shopkeeper. To avoid being the one that loses, neither side budges, so ultimately no deal is reached.

On the other hand, if you agree at 100 Dirham, in the middle, this is a compromise. It is a little bit more than the price you had in mind and a little less than what the shopkeeper was looking for. Both parties are slightly disappointed with the result.

Positional bargaining tends to result in either no deal, because the stand-off cannot be resolved, or in a compromise, in which neither side is fully happy.

Evil dolphins

Thanks to Flipper, we all think dolphins are nice, endorsed by the fact they smile and because we know of stories where they save a drowning swimmer by helping them back to shore. Goodness, even the film star Dick Van Dyke was recently saved by porpoises. (Had they *seen* his films?)

However, these are the stories we know of. We do not know of any stories of evil dolphins forcing swimmers away from shore because we simply would not hear of them, the victim would not be able to tell us.

This is known as the Survivorship Bias – we make our judgements purely on the evidence of the winners or survivors, ignoring those that were not so successful.

In the same way, Neanderthal negotiators who grunt their way through a deal, think they are good because they occasionally scare a softie into a big concession. But, if they are to be accurate about their abilities, they need to take into account the deals they do not get, as a result of them being too stubborn or too unpleasant.

Interest-based bargaining

Instead of focussing on fixed positions, another approach is to consider the interests of both parties. That is, what are they really trying to achieve, in the bigger picture?

John sat in his boss's office, knowing the meeting was going nowhere. "I'm sorry, John, I just can't give you a promotion with the way things are now, you're being unreasonable".

"*You're* being unreasonable. You promised me a promotion last year, I've still got the email, and I've gone way beyond my targets. If I can't feel I can trust you..."

"It's not me, I'd love to give you a promotion, believe me. It's the ruling – no more promotions. There's a headcount freeze, pure and simple. If I put you forward, they will just say no."

John felt betrayed. "Well, I'll have to look elsewhere. If you're not going to give me the reward for the work I've put in, I'll find someone who will."

There was a stand-off. They looked at each other in silence, both trying to think of a way forward but there just did not seem to be any. One side wanted something, the other would not give it. Who was going to break?

It was John who broke the silence, "I *deserve* a pay-rise and I deserve to sit on the Executive Board."

"Listen, I'd love to have you on the board, your input would be invaluable. That's not the issue, you can come along to our next meeting on Monday. Come along to all the meetings, it would be great. I can give you the pay-rise, as well. I just can't give you the title, there is a headcount freeze and it simply wouldn't be authorised."

"Well, I don't care about the title, you can call me whatever you like, I just want the recognition and the chance to input at a higher level."

"So if I sort out the pay-rise and I let the guys know that from Monday onwards, you'll be at the Executive Board meetings, will you be happy? I can get you a parking slot, as well, as it happens."

"That's perfect, that's all I want."

Both men sat back in their chairs and laughed, a little bit embarrassed. They were both pleased with the result. The stand-off was resolved without either giving in and both were happy with the outcome.

This is interest-based bargaining.

The initial positions involved were John wanting the promotion and his boss not being able to give it. These were mutually exclusive demands. At the level of position, there was a stand-off and no solution seemed possible.

However, when they moved to the level of interests, what did both parties *really* want, they were able to find a solution. John, as it turned out, was not interested in the job title, he was interested in a pay-rise and a place on the Executive Board. His boss was interested in keeping him in the company and was also interested in getting his input on the board. The deadlock was actually only with the job title, so by moving to interests they were able to find a solution.

Note, it did not involve compromise. This is a key point. Both sides obtained *fully* what they wanted.

Interests, are less likely to be mutually exclusive than positions and this is critical. It means there is far greater opportunity for a solution where both parties will be happy.

CHAPTER 2: THE STRONG WIN-WIN SYSTEM

If you are the kind that likes to skip the starters and main course and go straight to the dessert, here we will provide you with the bullet-pointed executive summary.

The logic of the Strong Win-Win system is:

1) Win-win is best even for selfish reasons because:
   a. Win-win creates extra value and your share of this is greater than if you took a win-lose approach.
   b. The negotiation counts for nothing unless it is implemented how you would like and, therefore, the other party must be incentivised to implement it as agreed.
2) However, many people are afraid of win-win because they feel it leaves them open to be taken advantage of. What is more, it only works if the other party adopts it too.
3) Therefore, use the Strong Win-Win system, which addresses these concerns.

Strong Win-Win involves strength and wisdom with an emphasis on both. Make sure you get your win, help them get their win. They are not independent.

And it boils down to four simple principles and a six-step method.

The Strong Win-Win Principles

1. It's not about winning the battle, it's about winning the war

This is self-evident but easy to forget. The implication is not to be too fixated on saving the cent here or you will miss the dollar over there. Focus on the bigger picture, get a bigger win.

2. In human endeavour, one plus one equals three

One idea plus one idea equals three ideas or more. You have a cow, I have a bull, together we have a business. When the output is greater than the sum of the inputs, this is value creation and it is this that has driven the whole progress of the human species.

3.   Never be rude to the waiter

They will do unspeakable things in your soup. The negotiation counts for nothing unless it is implemented the way you would like so make sure the other party is incentivised to do so.

4.   Be unmessable with!

When the lion lies down with the lamb we will all be happy. In the meantime, that lamb is going to have to find ways to do business with the lion without becoming lunch. So the lamb needs toughening up, then the lion ain't going to mess!

The first three of these principles show the value of win-win, even for selfish reasons. The last is there to ensure that you do not stray into lose-win.

And, armed with these principles, let us enter our negotiation with the six-step Strong Win-Win method.

The Strong Win-Win Method

1.   Prepare!

Let us put it simply: Olympic athletes spend four years preparing for one event, Sunday players stub out their cigarette and begin. Are you a Sunday player or are you a world-class professional?

2.   Develop your Plan B

Know *and develop* your alternatives. As the saying goes, "Never fall in love with one house, fall in love with three". And then you never have to be needy, you can never be bullied; you are always prepared to walk away if the deal is not right. This gives you a lot of power in the deal.

3.   Establish high credibility and high rapport

Establish high credibility and they will not mess with you. Establish high rapport and they will be pleased to help you get your win. With these in place, it is negotiating downhill.

4. Move them to win-win

Win-win only works if the other party is playing the same game. Many of the people you meet will default to win-win, others may need a helping hand. Show them the benefits of collaborating and talk in terms of their best interests. People respond in kind to your behaviour, so whatever behaviour you want to see, do it. They will reciprocate.

5. Solve the problem

Reframe the situation as a problem to be solved. It is not you against the counterparty, it is the two of you against the problem. Sharing resources, sharing ideas, sharing knowledge, working together to create value and help all parties achieve their win. It is not an arm-wrestle, it is an arm-game.

6. Trust but verify

Trust is good. There is a trust dividend and a lack-of-trust tax. But trust appropriately, do not be the fool that looks for fairness from a crocodile. The answer? Know how to tell if you can trust someone, know what to do to increase their trustworthiness and know what to do if you really cannot trust them at all.

Now, you may look at these and think there is something missing. Move them to win-win? How, exactly, do we do that, Simon? By magic? Solve the problem - again, by magic?

Well, yes, maybe there is magic. But, as Arthur C Clarke pointed out, any technology sufficiently far advanced will appear as magic.

So don't worry, we will give you the technology.

CHAPTER 3: THE STRONG WIN-WIN PRINCIPLES

Principle 1: It's not about winning the battle, it's about winning the war

This is self-evident but easy to forget; the key to long-run success is being clear about the bigger picture. The implication is not to be too fixated on saving the cent here or you will miss the dollar over there. Focus on the bigger picture, get a bigger win.

- Does the job title really make a difference if I am still walking away with a 20% pay rise and the new responsibilities mean I sit on the board?

- Do I really mind about the last £500 in the divorce settlement as long as it allows me to close an episode and move on with my life?

- Does this square metre of border territory really matter if conceding it (or giving it as a gift) enables us to live peacefully and prosper and plan a wealthier and happier future?

This is not to say forget the detail, often it is crucial. But it is to say put it into perspective, and if there is ever a conflict between the detail and the whole, the whole should always win.

Give a little, get a lot

In the 2010 United Kingdom general election there was an inconclusive result with neither Conservatives nor Labour, the two largest parties, winning a clear majority. There followed five days of frantic multi-lateral negotiations involving these two along with various minority parties and different factions within each party, all aimed at forming a stable coalition to govern the country. The nation held its breath.

The Liberal Democrats were the largest minority party and held the balance of power. They could work with either of the two

---

majors and form a coalition with enough seats to govern. Historically, they had been natural enemies of the Conservatives and their traditional allies were Labour.

Yet the talks resulted in a coalition between the two natural enemies. The Lib-Dems found themselves in bed with people they had spent their whole political lives fighting. How come?

Of course, there are many reasons why but one factor, in particular, became clear in interviews after the event. Liberal Democrat grandees, like Paddy Ashdown and Simon Hughes, all described exuberantly how the Conservatives handed out concessions like Santa at a shopping mall. They were amazed and thrilled at the policy gifts they were getting for free.

From a positional point of view, this is disastrous negotiation. Giving away things for free? Giving away things *hand-over-fist* for free?!

But the net result was that it enabled the Conservatives to achieve power, after 14 years in opposition, despite not having a majority. From a *bigger picture* point of view, the Conservatives scored a tremendous victory.

Had they been steadfast in their position and not budged an inch, they might have won a battle or two but they would have lost the war. Instead, they were quite happy to lose a few meaningless battles because, without question, it meant they won the war.

Principle 2: In the world of human endeavour, one plus one equals three

One idea plus one idea equals three ideas or more. You have a cow, I have a bull, together we have a business. When the output is greater than the sum of the inputs, this is value creation and it is this that has driven the whole progress of the human species.

Win-win comes from creating greater value

In 2010, Google wanted to launch an advertising service on mobile phones but the Monopolies Trust investigated the deal and were ready to block it. It was only when Apple also announced their move into the sector, and so introduced competition, that Google were allowed to proceed.

The extraordinary implication of this is that you can imagine certain circumstances where it may have been in Google's greater interests to have somehow subsidised Apple's deal. If Apple had been wavering, a helping hand from their rival might have provided sufficient impetus for them to go ahead. And in doing so, they would create a whole new market   generating extra value for everyone to share, including themselves.

Helping a competitor seems quite counter-productive. But this is not an arm-wrestle, this is the arm-game. Helping the other party in such a way that you gain too.

Win-win comes from creating greater value and you do this by looking at the bigger picture of each party.

Win-win – how do we do it?

All well and good but let us get practical: how do we actually do it in the deal?

Well, at its very simplest, ask:

- What do I want to achieve?
- What do they want to achieve?
- How can I help them achieve their win *in such a way that it helps me achieve mine?*

- Or, how can they help me achieve my *win in such a way that it helps them achieve theirs?*

Now, instead of trying to achieve your goal at the other's expense, both parties are working together to help achieve both parties' goals. Negotiated solutions do not have to be at anybody's expense. You have built a bridge between the two goals so everyone will be pulling in the same direction to get there.

Creating a bigger pie

A powerful approach is to find a way to create extra value.

Imagine you have a pie and you are negotiating between you how to divide it out.

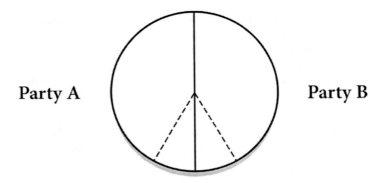

We could split it down the middle but if Party A wanted a larger slice of pie, it would necessarily be at the expense of Party B. Likewise, if Party B wanted a larger slice of pie. Such is the positional approach.

Another way is to ask the question "How can *both* parties get a larger slice at the same time?". The only way of doing this is to create a larger pie.

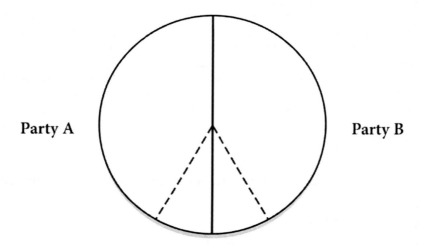

Party A   Party B

Now, even if there is a bit of wrangling at the end and one side gets more than half of the final pie, both sides achieve more than they would have originally.

In our earlier example, Google by themselves had no market; Google and Apple together had a market. New value was created by working together.

Cheating? No. Intelligent? You bet.

Win-win comes from creativity

So how do you create that larger pie? The first step is to move your thinking towards interests. At the bigger picture level, there is much more scope for creating greater value which can then be happily divided.

But a solution where all parties benefit is not necessarily apparent at first thought, so creative thinking is also required. If you want to bake a bigger pie, you may need to be inventive.

However, the corollary is also true – that a more creative solution usually does exist and the successful negotiator will look for this. A good negotiator always thinks beyond the obvious and works on the principle that there is likely to be more than one solution for every problem.

Negotiation is a highly creative process. If we carry on our culinary theme (and apologies if you are reading this page on an empty stomach), we can think of it as two people sharing their ingredients and together being able to make a much richer dish. If you have two or three things in your larder and I have two or three things in my fridge, the chances are that there are many more tasty options open to us together than there are individually. We may have to have a conversation to agree on the dish that we both like but it will almost certainly be better than what either of us could have produced with what we had by ourselves.

This is the whole basis of economic theory – individual interests plus trade equals greater value for all.

Win-win at work

In the 1980's, the film industry in Britain went through the doldrums which only turned around after a large-scale investment in new cinemas, particularly with the introduction of multiplexes.

The major film studios contributed to this investment because they saw the win-win value. By making cinemas nicer places to go, more people would go to see their films. Cinema companies and film studios both benefitted.

Deming, the management consultant and professor credited with a significant contribution to the post-war Japanese economic miracle, said "Your suppliers are what you make them" and there are many examples of Japanese manufacturers making their suppliers "better". This illustration from the film industry is an example of "Your distributors are what you make them".

Help your business partners be better. It is for your own good. Win-win at work.

Principle 3: Never be rude to the waiter

They will do unspeakable things in your soup! The negotiation counts for nothing unless it is implemented the way you would like so make sure the other party is incentivised to do so.

The important thing is the implementation

On 28th June, 1919, the Treaty of Versailles was signed to end World War I. Marshal Foch, the French Field Marshall, saw its limitations and declared "This is not peace. It is an armistice for 20 years." World War II broke out on 1st September, 1939. Foch was out by 65 days.

Win-lose has costs and perhaps the biggest cost comes from our original definition: that negotiations count for nothing unless they are implemented as agreed. So if you squeeze the other party in your negotiation, it is very likely they will sabotage the deal in its implementation and neither party will get what they wanted.

It is the principle of never being rude to the waiter. When you are in a restaurant, because of the nature of the relationship, you have it in your power to be as rude as you like to the waiter. You can refuse to leave a tip, you can swear and shout at them, you can call the manager over and rant and rage about how terrible the service was.

And they will smile and take it all politely and say "Certainly sir, my apologies sir" and then, back in the kitchen, they will do unspeakable things in your soup! Never be rude to the waiter!

You may squeeze your supplier to reduce his prices by 20% but to deliver at that price he will have to do less stringent quality checks or put junior staff on the project. You may get a great price from your customer because this time they are needy but you will never sell to them again. You may successfully strong-arm a clause into the contract but it simply will not be implemented.

And even if you get away with it this once, in the longer term it will come back to bite you. It is a small world and word gets around. You will get a reputation and you will miss out on all of the high value deals because people will learn not to deal with you.

Now, macho win-lose operators often brag how great and tough they are. But it is the same with that customer in the restaurant. He will be saying to all around, "Ha, I showed the way to deal with a waiter, didn't I?" but everyone else will be looking at each other knowingly.

Be fair, for selfish reasons

The Ultimatum Game is a much-studied game in the worlds of psychology and economics. In a typical game, £10 is to be divided between two people, Person A gets to choose how much goes to each person and Person B simply has the choice to accept or not accept. However, if they do not accept, *no one* gets anything.

Theoretically, Person B should accept any deal greater than zero because, after all, anything is better than nothing. However, in practice, Person B frequently vetoes the deal unless they think the split is fair.

Obviously, a 50-50 split is seen as fair and always accepted. But a 70-30 split, and sometimes even 60-40, is often considered unfair and Person B is prepared to hurt themselves in order to punish Person A for their unfairness.

The learning from this is clear: human beings have an innate sense of fairness which they consider important. Therefore, the negotiation must be seen as fair by all parties otherwise they will sabotage it, *even if it is against their own interests to do so.*

Principle 4: Be unmessable with!

When the lion lies down with the lamb we will all be happy. In the meantime, that lamb is going to have to find ways to do business with the lion without becoming lunch. So the lamb needs toughening up, then the lion ain't going to mess!

Put it on steroids, put it through a fitness training programme and teach it kung-fu. Crikey, get nuclear back-up if you need it. Then the lion will show respect. The lamb can still do its lamb-like things, knowing that if the lion tries to spoil its day, cute little lammikins will kick lion-ass!

Be unmessable with! Never bully but refuse to be bullied. Treat yourself with respect so that they too treat you with respect. Such is Strong Win-Win.

Win-win is absolutely the way forward but toughen yourself up to make sure that the other party does not take advantage.

We do not, repeat, we do not want to stray into lose-win.

Do not let yourself be bullied

How others rate relate to you partly depends on how you project yourself. If you sometimes find yourself being bullied, maybe there is something in how you are coming across. If you project assertiveness (assertive as opposed to passive or aggressive), it is far less likely to happen.

It is a key aspect of negotiation that you treat everyone with the respect that high status deserves. And that everyone includes you. Indeed, it can be very powerful to acknowledge their status and yours as equal ("You're an expert in your field, of course, and I'm an expert in mine..." or "We both know a lot about this industry...").

Be assertive. Not passive. Not aggressive.

Treating yourself and others with respect is about behaving assertively. Assertive behaviour is different to both being passive and to being aggressive.

Passive behaviour means not valuing yourself and not looking out for your rights or your outcome, instead letting the other party get theirs, often at your expense. This is a lose-win approach and is not a good negotiation tactic!

However, the answer is not aggressive behaviour. With aggressive behaviour you stop valuing the other party and you make sure you get your outcome, at the expense of theirs. This is win-lose and is not a sustainable negotiation tactic either.

Instead, assertive behaviour lies in between the two. It is win-win. Assertive people make sure they get their win but not at the expense of the other party's. Assertive behaviour values both parties' rights and objectives and works to achieve them.

If passive and aggressive are at the two ends of the spectrum, assertiveness lies in the middle. This can give you a good guideline as to what would be the correct response in any situation. Ask yourself:

- What would be a passive response here?
- What would be an aggressive response here?
- And therefore, what would be an assertive response here?

So imagine the scenario where your counterparty shouts furiously at you, "How dare you ask for this clause to be added to the contract, it's totally out of order! I demand you remove it straightaway!"

You are surprised and your first response is to get angry and shout back but then you realise that would be aggressive and would not necessarily get you your best result. Mentally, you go through some other options. "I could let him have his way, I suppose, and remove it." But you discard that option, too, for being unnecessarily passive. After all, there is a reason you put that clause in.

You decide to take the assertive route. "Well, I'd be grateful if we could talk about this in a normal tone of voice. I hear that you are angry this has been included and I'm sorry for that. There are very good reasons it is in there and I'm quite happy to discuss them. I'm also quite happy to talk about other ways of achieving the same ends, maybe there is a way that is more amenable to you which still satisfies my own outcomes."

Assertive. Not passive. Not aggressive.

The most important negotiation the world has ever seen

"I remember leaving the White House at the end of that Saturday. It was a beautiful fall day; and I remember thinking that I might never live to see another Saturday night".

So said American Secretary of Defence Robert McNamara, amidst the most important negotiation the world has ever seen.

With nuclear war imminent, the future of the world was balanced on a knife-edge.

October 1962. Kennedy had publicly called upon the Soviet Union to withdraw the missiles they had installed on Cuba and he had placed America's own nuclear missiles on ready alert with twenty planes in the air poised to launch an attack on the USSR.

Khrushchev's response was immediate and pugnacious, refusing to comply and placing his own ICBM nuclear strike force on high alert.

The fight is on. It is Wednesday, 24th October. Nearly three hundred American ships move into position on the quarantine line with instructions to use force on any Russian ship that refuses to halt. Twenty-five Soviet ships are sailing towards them, with submarine support. Khrushchev's order is for the ships to continue on their way and not stop. The American Navy will have to sink them to prevent them getting through.

Events accelerate. Russian troops in Cuba are put on standby and authorised to use tactical nuclear weapons if they think fit. A U-2 spy plane is shot down over Cuba. The U.S. Navy boards the Soviet ship Marucla for inspection. They drop depths charges on the Russian submarines, who are poised to launch nuclear torpedos in return.

Eyeball-to-eyeball. Pistols cocked. Hair trigger. Anything can happen. According to the Soviet General and Army Chief of Operations, Anatoly Gribkov, "Nuclear catastrophe was hanging by a thread … and we weren't counting days or hours, but minutes."

Kennedy does not want war but nor will he yield to what he saw as Russian bullying. As his brother Robert later said, "Every opportunity was to be given to the Russians to find a peaceful settlement which would not diminish their national security or be a public humiliation."

Khrushchev, it turns out, does not want war either. Like Kennedy, he sees the terrible danger of accidental Armageddon so when offered the chance to achieve his interests by different means, he takes it.

Kennedy promises he will respect Cuba's freedom and gives a secret promise to withdraw 15 US missiles stationed in Turkey, and Khrushchev agrees to withdraw the missiles from Cuba. The Soviet Defence Minister gives the order "Remove them as soon as possible. Before something terrible happens."

The world steps back from the brink.

CHAPTER 4: PREPARE!

4.1 YOUR WIN

Until now we have focussed on principles and definitions, concepts and theory. Now we are going to get practical. Very, very practical. But before we get stuck into the deal, there is one last thing we need to do.

Prepare.

Introduction

Those new to negotiation, who see it as an unfathomable art, often wish there is some magic trick they can pull off that will mysteriously deliver their best deal in all situations. It is the most commonly requested outcome from delegates on my courses.

Fortunately, such a trick exists. It is called preparation.

Many top negotiators believe that 75% of the skill is in the preparation. If you want to know what to do in the heat of the deal, as the deadline is looming and the other person is shouting at you and banging the table and your client is demanding you do not budge an inch, your best bet is to prepare.

The simple fact is that if you want to get the best deal you can, you need to prepare. When Richard Branson bought Necker Island, it was on the market for £3m and was way out of his budget. However, he did his research. He found that the owner, a British lord, was not actually very wealthy and needed £200,000 to build a house in London. Branson offered £200,000.

He got the island.

Perhaps even more compelling than that, if you do not prepare, you can be sure the other party will. And if they are inclined, they will take advantage of you and take you to the cleaners. A key part of the defensive aspect of Strong Win-Win is to know your stuff. If you want them to respect you, you have to be credible.

And once you have prepared sufficiently, the rest is negotiating downhill.

The dangers of complacency

We can all be seduced into complacency. We have done this type of deal many times before or we think our natural skills or experience will easily handle the other party. This is a recipe for regret.

In 1977, Ed Roberts sold his computer hardware company, MITS, to Pertec for $6.5 million. In actual fact, MITS' revenue was no longer coming from the hardware but primarily from software they licensed which had been written by a couple of teenage programmers.

The programmers were disputing the licence and trying to regain ownership of it, which would massively reduce the value of the deal if they were successful. Pertec were not worried, they had a large legal department that would deal with speed-bumps such as this, and they continued with the acquisition. They then sent their chief counsel to deal with the straightforward matter of the young software guys.

One of the programmers was called Paul Allen, the other was called Bill Gates, the fledgling company Microsoft. People outside the meeting room described the screaming and shouting they heard. It did not go as smoothly as Pertec expected. The dispute went to arbitration. Pertec lost and were left with $6.5m worth of nothing. Gates and Allen went on to make billions of dollars from their software rights. Ed Roberts, sometimes called the grandfather of computing, would maintain years later that the software that helped Gates and Allen become billionaires rightfully belonged to MITS and therefore Pertec.

Such are the dangers of complacency.

So how much should you prepare and what should you cover?

The simple answer is whatever is necessary to get the deal. Any surprises and you did not do enough preparation.

The world of sports is an interesting arena for two reasons. Firstly, it is a massive industry with huge amounts of money resting on success or failure. Secondly, it is supremely measurable: you win or you lose, you score more goals than the other team or you do not, you jump higher than the other athlete or you do not.

So how much preparation do sportsmen and women put in? The answer is: it depends. Olympic athletes spend four years preparing for one event. Four years preparation for one event! At the other end of the spectrum, Sunday players stub out their cigarette then start to play.

In sports, Sunday players do not prepare, professionals do. Are you a Sunday player or a professional?

And what do you need to cover in your preparation? The answer is the same: whatever is necessary to win the deal.

So have a very clear idea of what you would like from the deal. But spend just as much time looking at it from their side of the table. Hey, there are two people in this conversation. Actually, there are probably more than two, and you need to cover it from everyone's perspective. So take the time to consider anyone who may impact or may be impacted by the deal and look at it from their point of view too.

So let us go through it in that order – you, them, everybody else.

What do you want to get from the deal?

The very first question to ask as part of the preparation is what you would like to achieve from the deal. But, as we have seen, we need to answer this at the level of the bigger picture.

One method to reveal the bigger picture is to ask "What do I want to achieve?" and then ask "Why do I want to achieve that?". Repeat the second question as many times as feels right.

I worked with the purchasing department of a large company in the space industry. Before they entered any negotiations with a supplier, their starting point was to remind themselves of who they were as a company, what their vision and values were and what they were trying to achieve as an organisation.

From *there*, they were able to make sure that any deal they agreed took them towards those bigger picture goals.

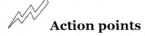 **Action points**

Before you start your negotiation, take a step back and ask:

▸ What is your bigger, long-term goal?
▸ What are you really trying to achieve from this deal?
▸ Why do you want to achieve that?
▸ How does this negotiation fit into the bigger picture?

Then at all times in the negotiation, consider how you are on track to achieving this bigger goal and use it as your benchmark.

What is your ideal outcome?

Getting the cheapest price is by no means incompatible with achieving your bigger picture. Interests and positions are not mutually exclusive but you should start from the broader perspective and, from there, zoom in to the details.

Needless to say, there is likely to be a range of outcomes that you would be happy with and it is worthwhile taking the time to consider what would be your ideal outcome.

When it comes to your annual pay review, you may think a 10% rise would be nice. But what about a 20% rise? Or an upgrade in your car? Or a stake in the equity? These would be nicer still, wouldn't they? Don't ask, don't get.

Many people do not achieve the best deal available to them because they do not think to ask.

Never negotiate yourself down before you even talk with the other party! This is a very common mistake. Ask for what you want and you may be pleasantly surprised. Indeed, they will take you more seriously for doing so. We cannot rely on our counterparties to be as automatically generous as we would like, sometimes they need our help.

So take the time to think what would be an ideal outcome from the negotiation then ask for it. Set yourself a stretch target, one that you would really be happy with. Studies have consistently shown that those who enter negotiations with higher aspirations attain better outcomes.

Of course, your stretch target must be justifiable. Consider the concept of your Maximum Plausible Position. This is the highest position you can ask for without losing credibility. Do not be afraid of asking for this but be prepared to provide reasons.

What is the minimum that is still worthwhile for you?

It is also very important to know the minimum you would accept. But, again, not from a positional point of view but from the perspective of your interests.

If you are selling your old car, say, your positional approach might say "I won't accept anything less than £2,000 for it". But if someone were to give you their motorbike and £1500 cash, this might be worthwhile after all, even though it is less than your bottom line. On the other hand, if you need the money to spend on a new kitchen, then £2,000 really should be your minimum. Unless, of course, they are a kitchen-fitter...

So at all times, use your interests as your guideline.

What is the best way for knowing whether a deal is worthwhile or not? Compare it to your Plan B. If it is one penny better, go for it; one penny worse, duck out. Knowing and developing your Plan B is so important that we will dedicate a whole chapter to it.

 Action points

Having identified how this negotiation fits in with your bigger picture, ask:

- What is your bigger, long-term goal?
- What would be an ideal outcome from the negotiation?
  - What is your Maximum Plausible Position?
- What are your reasons for this MPP?
- What is your minimum?

Break it down into the detail

The clearer your outcome, the more likely you are to achieve it. This means it is important to go into the details. Negotiations are very rarely one-dimensional, they are nearly always more complex and identifying the details of the different variables involved will give you greater power.

For example, it is much easier to reduce your telephone bill if it is itemised. Armed with an itemised bill you can see exactly where you spend your money and which calls to reduce to achieve most savings.

In a house purchase the obvious variable is price but there can be many more involved: deposit, cash payment or mortgaged, inclusion of furniture and fittings, date of exchange, date of completion, date of moving, repairs or enhancements made before or after purchase and many, many others. Other negotiations could include many more variables. The more creative you are, the more variables you will be able to identify.

It is important to know your preferred outcome for each of these variables and also, if relevant, the minimum that you would accept.

Prioritise

And then prioritise. This is key. It is through prioritisation that you make sure you get the things that are the most important to you.

There are different ways to prioritise but all involve using your bigger picture goals as your reference point. The simplest way is to categorise the variables by:

- must have
- nice to have
- not too fussed about.

Alternatively, you can be more meticulous and rank them in numerical order.

Of course, it is not always easy to compare things that are of a different nature. Which is more important to you – that the property has four bedrooms or that it has a large garden? Or that it is close to a good school? Or that your commute to work is simple?

One way of making this easier is to put monetary figures to them. If there were two houses next to each other in identical condition and one had three bedrooms and the other four, how much more money would you pay for the fourth bedroom? Do a similar exercise for each of the different variables. That will give a very rough estimate of their value to you. By putting them in the same units of measurement, it makes it easier to prioritise.

Identifying the variables gets your best deal

It is important to identify all of the variables because it enables you to get your best deal.

Suppliers may try to dazzle you with a great price but re-coup their margin in other ways. Being aware of the full details of the deal will arm you against this.

Alternatively, you may have an important customer trying to push your price down and squeeze your margin. Broadening out the negotiation is your answer. Identifying the different variables gives you scope to meet their headline price demands whilst still achieving a viable return overall.

The other benefit of itemising the different variables is to identify where the easy trades are to be made. We shall see the power of this in the next section.

 **Action points**

Break the deal down into its details. Question everything. This is a creative process.

▸ What are the different variables involved?

▸ What are your preferred outcomes for each?

▸ Use the bigger picture goals as your benchmark to prioritise between the variables.

Do your research

To evaluate your best outcome, and best route towards that outcome, you will need to research the situation.

Do whatever due diligence is necessary to ensure your calculations and reasoning are correct. The more guess-work or assumptions are involved the more likely you are to be surprised in the meeting.

Double check what you are told. Even sources within your own team can be unreliable. The client you are representing may tell you "facts" which are not actually true. It could be wishful thinking on their part or a 'selection' of relevant points or a re-construction of events based on assumptions and prejudices that will distort the story. Cross-check every point from as many sources as you can.

There may be gaps in the facts that still need clarification and identify assumptions that may be incorrect.

All of these should be verified *before* the negotiation rather than getting caught out during or, worse, after the negotiation.

Be a SWOT!

The SWOT analysis is a classic tool for assessing the bigger picture. It is a methodical approach to reveal the positives and the negatives of both the present and the future. Take a sheet of paper and, from the point of the view of the negotiation, write down:

- your **S**trengths
- your **W**eaknesses
- the potential **O**pportunities
- and the potential **T**hreats.

This will give you a very good context for developing a strategy for the negotiation.

But don't leave it at that, see if there are ways of turning the weaknesses into strengths or the threats into opportunities. Take your cue from Elvis. The first time he performed to a live audience, when he was 19, he was so nervous his left leg shook visibly. At the break, he came off the stage and asked the producer why the girls were screaming. "They're going crazy for your leg! It's driving them wild, don't stop!" He went back on and shook the other leg too.

 **Action points**

Do your due diligence, assume nothing is reliable. Ask yourself:

▸ What research do I need to do?
▸ What assumptions are involved in my case?
▸ How can I verify these?
▸ What are my strengths, weaknesses, opportunities and threats?

4.2 THEIR WIN

So we know what we want from the deal. But that is not enough. Fundamental to a successful deal is taking the time to see the world from the other side of the table.

I want to repeat that exact sentence, to stress how important it is: fundamental to a successful deal is taking the time to see the world from the other side of the table.

And how they see it will be quite different to your perspective, that you can guarantee.

If we want to improve as a negotiator we need to shift our focus to their point of view. Why? Because we have spent a lifetime looking at the world from our point of view. But we have persuaded ourselves already! If it was only us, there would be no negotiation. To influence the other side to come to a profitable deal, we need to see things how they do.

Let us look at a typical sales situation. Selling is by no means the only type of negotiation but we can use it to illustrate a point. In sales there are two worlds at play. The first world is the world of the salesperson and it involves the salesperson, their product and the customer.

Product   Salesperson   Customer

And the salesperson spends a lot of time talking about their wonderful product to the customer, describing all of its great features and amazing capabilities. Especially if it really is a wonderful product. And they do not get the sale. Why not?

Because the customer's world is very different.

The customer's world consists of their boss (who is giving them grief), their team (who are giving them grief), their other colleagues (who are giving them grief), their own customers (who are giving them lots of grief), their other suppliers (who are giving them grief), their partner and their children (who are giving them huge amounts of grief) and...well, you get the picture.

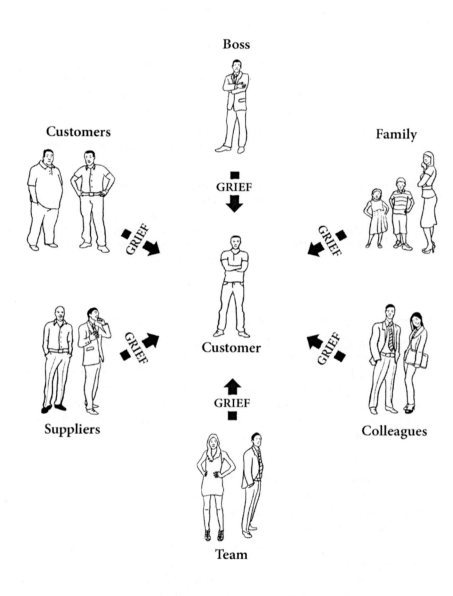

The customer's world is very different to the salesperson's. The salesperson is not in it at all or maybe registers as a small annoying blip. The customer certainly is not interested in the product on offer. All they are thinking about is all of the problems they are facing from everyone else who is giving them so much grief!

What the customer wants to buy is a magic wand that will magic all the problems away. If the salesperson is selling magic wands, great. If not, they have to step into the shoes of the customer and see this picture from their point of view. They will then begin to understand these problems and be able to see how their product might help solve one of them.

And then, and only then, will the customer think about buying the product because all they are really interested in is getting their problems fixed.

Likewise in any negotiation. If you want to reach a successful resolution, take the time to step into the world of the other party and see things from their angle. After all, you are asking them to shift their thinking, it would only be courteous to shift your own thinking to their perspective first. Once you have done this, you will begin to understand your negotiating counterparty's point of view more fully. And now you can ask the same questions regarding their outcome as you did of yours.

Know Your Counterparty Better Than They Do

If you are a salesperson, the best approach is to know your customer better than they do. Know *their* customers, their competitors, their industry, their issues. If you are a purchaser, the best approach is to know your supplier better than they do. If you are a lawyer, know your counterparty better than they do. If you are a diplomat, know the other country better than they do. If you are a regulator, know your industry practitioners better than they do.

You get the idea.

So do the research. Find out their situation, their constraints, their long-term aspirations, their company guidelines, their internal politics, their personal feelings, their strengths and weaknesses, their market trends and their competition.

How do they see *you*? How do they see your strengths and weaknesses? What are the difficult issues they are going to ask you about? If there are any, prepare your answers to these especially. Answering in the heat of the moment, unprepared, may not produce the best responses. However, now, in your preparation time, when you have the space to develop a considered response, you will think of something much more intelligent.

Get deeper into their world by asking a friend or colleague to join you in a role-play. You "become" your counterparty, and let your friend ask "you" questions. This will undoubtedly give you great insight. Alternatively, ask your friend or colleague to role-play your counterparty. Again, you will get fresh insights into what drives them.

Quite apart from shedding light on their perspective, this research may well give a different angle to your own argument. Maybe your client has not told you the whole truth. Maybe your figures are not quite as robust as you thought they were. Maybe you will new see ways of creating extra value or reaching win-win.

Develop a powerful horse manure detector

In days long ago, a knight lived and died with his horse. The Spanish word for nobleman, caballero, comes directly from their word for horse. They knew their horses.

Indeed, they knew their horse manure. If they came across some, they would pick it up and sniff it. Why?

From its odour, they could tell the horse's diet. Had it been eating grass? Or oats? This was highly important information. If it had been eating grass, the likelihood the horse was wild. If it had been eating oats, it was not a wild horse, it was a war horse.

And if it was a war horse and not yours, there was an enemy in the area.

What has this to do with negotiation? A lot. There is information out there to be found in the unlikeliest of sources. And it can make the difference between life and death, between getting your deal and not getting it. Sniff it out!

I consulted for one company who were bidding for a multi-billion pound contract. They told me that as part of their preparation, they had found out who the key decision-maker was going to be. Good, I was impressed. But it did not stop there.

They found out her address. They found out the route of her commute to work. They found out the billboards that stood on the sides of that commute to work. They found out the company that leased those billboards and they were now in the middle of putting together an advertising campaign that would sit nicely on them! I was very impressed.

Do your research, know your counterparty, it can make all the difference.

 Action points

How does it look from their side of the table?

▸ Research as much as you can about their situation using all of the different sources

▸ Do a SWOT analysis (see above) on their position

▸ Step into their shoes as wholly as you can, how does this deal look from this perspective?

What is their bigger picture?

In exactly the same way that the first question you asked of yourself was "What is your bigger picture and how does this negotiation fit with that?", your first question of the other party should be "What is *their* bigger picture?". In the long-term, what do they want? And how can this negotiation help them achieve this?

You may ask why care about their longer-term goals? Because it is in this way we create the greater value that makes the win-win process so effective. This is how *you* get your best deal. This is what turns the process from an arm-wrestle where your energies cancel each other out to the arm-game where your energies work with each other to maximise value for all parties.

So find out their bigger picture and consider how this deal can help them achieve that.

Find out their drivers

J.P. Morgan said that people buy for very good reasons, and then there is the real reason. It is this real reason that you want to discover because this is where most leverage lies.

The very good reasons are likely to be solid business grounds and the kind of thing that everybody would agree is worthy. However, the real reason may be something quite individual and quite personal. It is unlikely that they will tell you what it is. To help uncover this, try to understand as much as you can about:

- their world
- their history
- their goals
- their personal drivers.

If you can crack this, you will have real leverage for your deal.

Let us take an example for illustration: you have just completed a friendly sale with the operations team of a large manufacturing firm and they are now replaced by the Chief Purchasing Officer to finalise the terms. As he enters the room, the temperature seems to drop and condensation appears on the inside of the window. He is built like a bull and he makes Mike Tyson look effeminate. He shakes your hand and your fingers crack. He slowly starts the squeeze. The price goes down and down.

Fine. Find out his real, personal drivers and work with those and in return find ways to make it worthwhile for you too. Ask him if his job targets are price reductions. It is almost certainly the case. Give him his headline price reduction (so he gets his bonus) but get increased volume in return or get him to hold the stock or separate out the delivery costs or whatever other win is available for you. Help him win his game but in such a way that you win your game too.

Or find out about *his* boss. If you can help him look good in front of his boss he will help you get your win in exchange.

Remember, deep down, people are very superficial. That deep, hidden, compelling driver is usually quite superficial: I want an easy life; I want to get that promotion; I want that trip to Marbella; I want to impress my boss; I want to impress my customer; I want to look good back in the office. Find this out, link it to your message, and you have a deal.

And, of course, always be diplomatic. Maybe asking him his job targets is too blunt (and you do not want to annoy him!) but work on that assumption. Verbalise the good reasons, imply the real reasons and let them make the connection for themselves.

Present your case in terms of benefits to them

Once you know your and their interests, these are your reference points that you continuously measure any proposition against. The success of your deal is not dependent on the price you get but on how it helps you achieve your bigger picture. And reminding them of their bigger picture will help you achieve that.

It is said that WIIFM is a radio station that everybody is tuned into all of the time and if you want to get your message across you need to broadcast on this wavelength, otherwise they will not hear you.

WIIFM, of course, stands for "What's In It For Me?"

Simon Horton   62

Whatever it is that you want to achieve, frame it in terms of what they want. Make it explicit. Ideally, they will see it for themselves anyway but do not rely on this. If they do not seem to be making the obvious conclusions, help them do the thinking. Talk them through it, take them through the calculations, so they can not avoid seeing the benefits for themselves.

Do the thinking for them

I worked with the sales team of a large German company manufacturing capital machinery. One of the team complained he lost a lot of custom to cheaper Japanese imports. He thought his customers were not buying intelligently because his products lasted longer and were therefore cheaper in the long-term. Moreover, they produced higher quality work, enabling his customers to charge higher prices to *their* customers and therefore make greater profit.

I asked him did he truly believe that his product was best value-for-money in the long-term for these reasons. He answered, "Yes". I asked him could he back that up with figures. He answered, "Give me a customer and give me about an hour and, yes, I could". I asked him had he ever done this for a customer. He answered, "No".

We met about six months later and he was now doing the calculations for his customers and getting the sales.

Do not expect them to make the inferences themselves, you often have to do the thinking for them.

Inspire them

If you want to motivate them, inspire them! As Antoine St-Exupéry said, "If you want to build a ship, don't call together some men just to gather wood, prepare tools and distribute tasks. Instead, teach them the longing for the endless sea". Relate it to the bigger picture and the goals that inspire them.

In the Northern Ireland peace process, whenever progress looked to be in the balance, George Mitchell would exhort the different parties to the very highest values and to the historic nature of what they were doing. In doing so, he would give it that extra momentum to proceed. And on the very last day of the process, as each party contemplated whether to support it or not, Bill Clinton stayed up through the night, talking to all the leaders on the telephone to inspire them towards a historic deal.

The most powerful motivating force in the world is the idea. People will give up their lives for an idea, let alone a clause in the contract. Inspire them.

 **Action points**

Think of it from their point of view and ask yourself:

▸ What is their bigger picture and how does this negotiation fit with that?

▸ What is their real driver in this deal?

▸ What is the WIIFM here?

▸ How can you inspire them?

Identify their priorities

It is unlikely you will prioritise your outcomes in exactly the same way as the other party and this can provide opportunity for an agreement.

You may be able to concede something that is of low priority to you but of high priority to them in return for something that is of high priority to you but of low priority to them and everyone is happy. This is another of the ways that the win-win approach creates extra value for all parties concerned.

There could be all kinds of reasons why they may have different priorities: different higher level objectives, different strengths and weaknesses, different time-scales, different appetites for risk, a different tax status, affected by different regulations, different constituency demands, geographical requirements, liquidity levels, preference for relationships, accounting periods and a million other possibilities.

So, you will already have ascribed your priorities, now do the same for the other party. What are the must-haves for them and what are the nice-to-have's?

Then look at the two lists, in order of importance, and see where the differences are. Which variables are important to one side but not to the other?

Now you can create value. Now you can trade. We are in win-win territory already.

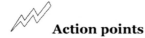 **Action points**

Think of it from their point of view and ask yourself:

▸ What would be an ideal outcome for them?
▸ How do they prioritise the different variables?
▸ Where are the possibilities for trading?
▸ What is the minimum that is of value for them?

Expect deadlock

Expect deadlock, it is a natural part of the negotiation process. Plan for it. Now you have prepared your own desired outcomes and you have researched their likely objectives, consider where the possible stand-offs may be.

And then be creative in developing solutions for them so that you can deal with them if and when they arise.

Later in the book we spend more time looking at several ways to resolve deadlocks and if you build sufficient rapport and trust with the other party they should be dealt with very easily. But it is certainly worth preparing for them in advance.

Know their culture

There is a famous story (which may be apocryphal) of an advertising campaign run by Coca-Cola in Saudi Arabia. The advert was a series of drawings, with no captions, and the idea was that the drawings spoke for themselves.

The first drawing was a picture of a man dying of thirst in the searing heat of the Saudi desert sun. The second was of the same man coming across a Coca-Cola vending machine. And the third was of that man, with the Coca-Cola in his hand, looking rejuvenated, re-vitalised and refreshed.

Unfortunately, the campaign was not successful. In fact, it became a laughing-stock. The reason? Arabs read from right to left so the advert they saw was of a healthy, energetic man drinking Coca-Cola and as a result dying of thirst!

Such is the importance of knowing the other party's culture.

It is beyond the scope of this book to go into great detail on this matter other than to highlight its importance. And we are not restricting it to geographical boundaries either. The culture in a bond-trading room will be very different to the culture in a convent. Even within the same organisation, cultures can be very different in different departments or different offices.

So make the effort to learn their culture, the last thing you want to do is nod your head for "yes", when in their culture nodding the head means "no way!".

At the same time, realise that the person you are dealing with is an individual and may not fit with the stereotype.

If there are cultural differences, *expect* miscommunications and allow for them.

And the best way to resolve cultural issues? Get face-to-face. Bring it back to human meeting human and it is amazing what difficulties can be resolved.

 **Action points**

Think of it from their point of view and ask yourself:

▸ Where might there be a potential deadlock? What might be a solution?

▸ What aspects of their culture do I need to be aware of?

A caveat

There is a strong caveat regarding all that has been said in the last few pages.

For all of the effort you put into understanding the world of the other party and seeing it from their perspective, any conclusion you come to from this process can only ever be *a guess*.

And, as such, that guess can be wrong. When you go into your meeting, be prepared for your surmises to be incorrect and your strategy to have to change.

It is very important to do this preparation and to understand the world from their point of view. But be prepared to throw it all out when it comes to the meeting itself.

4.3 MULTI-PARTY NEGOTIATIONS

Negotiations are never the simple two-party model.

It may be lawyer to lawyer, each representing a client or there may be a broker or consultant or mediator involved. There may be teams. There may be factions within the teams and coalitions across parties. Each will have different agendas and there may be several conversations going on at the same time. Some influencers will be present, others will influence from afar; some will be active and directly involved, some will be indirect and passively involved. And all of this can change (agendas, coalitions, personnel, engagement, circumstances) as the negotiation proceeds.

How do you chart your way through such complexity? More interestingly, complexity creates opportunity so how can you actively *use* it to your advantage?

The Northern Ireland peace process

Let us take the Northern Ireland peace process as a case in point.

In the talks that finally led to the Good Friday agreement in Northern Ireland, they directly involved 10 political parties, 2 national governments and three mediators. Each party had para-military bodies associated with them and various sub-groupings with significant tensions between those internal factions. The governments themselves had their own political concerns and, indeed, the ruling parties changed during the timescales of the process.

The discussions took years and, needless to say, many things changed in the world during those years, many things that impacted the negotiation itself. Political parties gained and lost power, individuals died and were replaced by new people, economic and social changes all had an effect.

There were the talks. And how these proceeded had been agreed in prior talks about the talks. And even how these were to proceed had been agreed in many years of less formal discussions between the key players – talks about talks about talks.

There were several loose groupings that would negotiate separately between themselves. The Catholic parties and the Irish government would meet; the Protestant parties and the British government would meet; and the two national governments would meet outside of the formal negotiation.

The mediators (one a Canadian, chosen by the British government; another a Finn, chosen by the Irish government; and a third an American of Irish-Arab descent, chosen by Bill Clinton) would have many conversations, often not with the decision-makers but their key representatives, sounding different scenarios and likely responses before the actual summit meetings themselves.

And even this is a high-level treatment. Zooming in only reveals more complexity.

Negotiations are never simple, static, one-to-one situations.

Different agendas within a team

Your negotiations may not be quite as complicated as the Northern Ireland situation but it is unlikely to involve the immediate other party and no-one else.

As soon as we have more than one person on a particular side of a table, that is a team and within teams different players will have different agendas. Some people will pull towards a negotiated deal, others will not. This requires negotiation between the members of the *same* team. Make sure they are done before you meet your counterparty and make sure everyone on your side is incentivised by the final agreement.

If not, it can seriously undermine your strategy. Senior FBI negotiator Gary Noesner describes this danger in a hostage situation: "Just when we had finally established a bond of trust with the perpetrator, moving closer to ending the crisis, we'd sometimes find that a fellow agent or police officer had thrown a rock through the window, ordered a military vehicle driven up on the lawn as a show of force, or turned off the power. This often produced violent resistance and injuries or death that might have been avoided".

Similarly, a study conducted by UMIST, the UK Institute of Logistics and A.T. Kearney, examined how companies worked in partnership with each other. It noted that often effective partnerships were formed at the operational level but they would get sabotaged when the sales and purchasing departments got involved. The commercial teams would undermine strong effective partnerships already formed and working. Make sure all factions of your team are working as one.

On the other hand, differences in agenda within the other team can create a multi-dimensional aspect which provides you with more opportunity for a deal.

They are not one indivisible unit. There will be a team at the table and they will report back to a boss or a senior management team or a client. There will be other colleagues and departments and customers and suppliers and impacted constituents, all of whom will have different agendas and attitudes and values and may have the power to affect the deal.

Each extra dimension provides extra opportunity for a deal or possibility for it breaking down.

Why were the Oslo Accords Unsuccessful?

The Oslo Accords between Israel and Palestine in 1993 were considered a great success at the time and hopes were very high for a lasting peace in the Middle-East. Unfortunately, the implementation was completely unsuccessful.

Why?

Obviously, there will be many reasons for the failure of such a complicated situation but one of the main factors was the disconnect between those people who negotiated the agreement and those who had to implement it.

Inside the negotiation room the different parties had built a good relationship, a trust, an appreciation of the other side making an effort, an understanding of the nuances of the agreement, an understanding of the spirit of the agreement.

Unfortunately, outside of the room, none of these existed. And it was the people outside of the room who were responsible for the implementation.

Greater care needed to be taken to ensure the different constituencies involved in the implementation, outside of the negotiation room, also owned and bought into the agreement and would therefore work toward its success.

Changing World

To add an extra dimension of complexity, negotiations are rarely static either. The world changes as the negotiation proceeds and this can impact the negotiations themselves. The North Vietnamese recognised this in 1968 when peace talks began between themselves and the Americans in Paris. The American team booked themselves into a hotel near the negotiation venue; the North Vietnamese rented an apartment on a two year contract. There were U.S. presidential elections due later in the year, they knew what they were doing.

The world is changing. And changing faster. According to Erik Qualman, author of Socialnomics, this is how long it took the following technologies to reach an audience of 50 million people:

- Radio: 38 years
- Television: 13 years
- Internet: 4 years

- iPod: 3 years
- Facebook: 2 years.

As the world changes, agendas change; strengths and weaknesses change, personnel change. These changes can impact your negotiation even as it proceeds.

Understanding the real dynamics of the deal

So if the issue we face is complexity and change, how do we manage it? And, one step further, how can we use it to our advantage?

The very first thing to do is identify who are all the different constituents that need to be borne in mind; who can impact the deal and who can be impacted. From here, identify who are the key decision-makers and who are the key influencers and start to develop an idea of the relationships between them.

Now, we started our preparation by clarifying our own desired outcomes and our bigger picture goals and we then did the same for other party. If we want to understand what is really going on in a negotiation, we need to do the same for each of the key players in the deal. If we need their buy-in, we need to know what will get that buy-in.

When Mahatma Gandhi negotiated with the Raj over the governance of India, before each meeting he would set a table and lay out a place for all of the important attendees. He would, in turn, sit at each seat and imagine himself to be that delegate and would look around the table from that perspective. He would ask himself what he (as that delegate) wanted and did not want to happen. He would ask himself what he (as that delegate) thought about all the other delegates there. It would give him a real feel for the forces in operation around the table and how he could best leverage those forces to his gain.

Mapping out the system visually

Of course, if there are a lot of people involved this can become quite complicated. It can be difficult to keep track of them all in your head, they never stand still! So, relieve your headache by getting it out of your head and on to paper.

A picture tells a thousand words and we can get great insight into the dynamics of a deal by mapping the situation visually. It reveals the important relationships involved and the key lines of force at work.

Let us take the simplest scenario where it really does seem to be a one-to-one conversation: you and the person on the other side of the table/phone/email/letter/courtroom/bedroom or bathroom door.

Even here there is complexity. Who is their boss and what do they want? Who is their wife or husband and what do they want? Who are the other key people in their life and what do these people want? What are they trying to achieve and what problems are they facing?

Get a piece of paper and put it all down. How good are you at drawing? Feel free to put as much artistic flair into it as you like! Use colour, use arrows, use different symbols to represent those who are for the deal and those who are against, use different symbols to represent those who can impact it and those who are impacted by it.

I will let you into a secret: I am crap at drawing! But it still works for me. I draw stick-men on the back of an envelope and I get results. It is not an exact science. Various software packages and stakeholder mapping tools exist to help you. You can take it to the level of formality, detail and scope you wish.

Who do you include on your map and where do you stop? Include anyone who will be impacted by the deal and anyone who can impact it. Comprehensiveness is not always necessary or helpful. We could extend the map forever if we had to. Instead, it is better to be led by pragmatism. And it will evolve. It is likely to be a "living" document – as the negotiation proceeds, you may need to change or add to it.

A simple example

I was involved in a negotiation with a major oil company and I was getting a constant "No" from the other side of the table, despite the obvious benefits for them from the deal.

So I took some paper and pens and drew out the map.

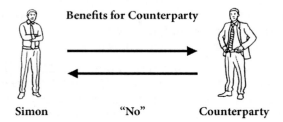

I realised that the "No" was not coming from the people I was talking to but they were simply following orders from above. I did not know who "Above" were but I did know they based in the American office. So I added them to the map.

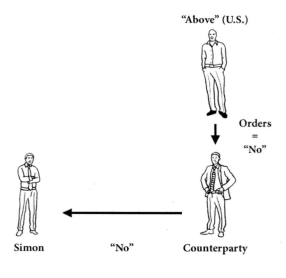

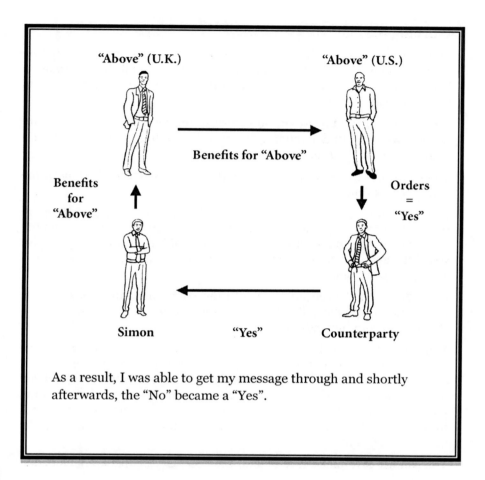

As a result, I was able to get my message through and shortly afterwards, the "No" became a "Yes".

Working the map

The military have their war-room, hostage negotiators use situation boards, either way it is the same concept – to have all the information laid out in a highly visual manner. And then there are many ways in which you can work with it.

You can use it to understand how best to influence the person you are dealing with. By understanding the world they live in, you will find a better way to fit your message to it.

You can use it to see where extra value can be created and so make the win-win apparent.

You can use it to create allies and build your power by getting more people on board, especially influential people. You can use it to identify who those influential people might be. These allies can support you, give you information, connect you to other people, exert pressure and champion your idea.

If people are not even entering into the communication, they are not responding to phone calls or emails, you can use it to identify indirect channels of communication.

You can use it to seed your ideas before the negotiation. If your idea is a new one or different to the other party's current thinking, you cannot expect them to change their mind easily. You will get better results if you do some work outside of the negotiation room. Sell your ideas to other people who you know will mention them to your target. If they hear it from two or three different sources before they meet you, they will be much more receptive.

You can use it to make sure that all the necessary people are included in the talks.

The Failure of the Copenhagen Climate Change Conference

In the United Nations Climate Change Conference that took place in Copenhagen in December 2009, all of the heads of state met in the final Summit meeting to bash out an accord.

However, according to Mark Lynas who was in the room representing the Maldives, one key individual who was not present was the Chinese Prime Minister, Wen Jiabao, "instead sending a second-tier official in the country's foreign ministry to sit opposite Obama himself. The diplomatic snub was obvious and brutal, as was the practical implication: several times during the session, the world's most powerful heads of state were forced to wait around as the Chinese delegate went off to make telephone calls to his superiors."

The "second-tier official" could not make important decisions and ultimately this led to the conference being unable to reach a meaningful agreement.

Negotiating Backwards

David Lax and Professor James Sebenius of Harvard Business School have devised the concept of 'negotiating backwards' as a way of tackling complex, multi-party, dynamic situations.

In their excellent book, "3-D Negotiation", their advice is to map out all of the people involved (as above), and identify the key person you ultimately need to get on board to achieve your goal.

Then work backwards from there – in order to get this person on board, what do you need to do? Who else do you need to get on board? And so on: keep working backwards until you have your strategy. At the end of this process, you will have a route-map to navigate your way, even as the situation evolves.

And with each of the people on that route, you need to address their bigger picture goals and their WIIFM considerations to get leverage.

War-gaming

Another approach is war-gaming. Instead of 'negotiating backwards', walk the negotiation through, going forwards. Who is going to open? With what? What is the response going to be? What will be the response to the response?

Run a timeline in parallel for each party involved and you will get an insight into how it will unfold. This is called war-gaming. If the situation is important enough, it is worth doing this.

 **Action points**

Negotiations are never simple, one-to-one matters, there is always value from considering a broader view.

▸ Map out all the people involved in the "system" of the negotiation and include everyone who may be impacted, directly or indirectly

▸ Who are the key players? What are their goals, their drivers?

▸ Identify all the influential players and potential allies or champions

▸ Work backwards from your end objective to identify your best strategy for the negotiation.

4.4 PREPARING YOURSELF

Self-awareness – a framework for wisdom

Is the glass half-full or half-empty? It all depends on how you frame it. Take a full glass of water and pour half of it out, 69% people will say the glass is half-empty. Take an empty glass and fill it up to half-way, 88% will say it is half-full.

And compare "Smoking increases your chances of death in the next 20 years from 1% to 1.3%" with "Smoking increases your chances of death in the next 20 years by 30%".

In both instances: identical data, different presentation, very different impact.

The human brain is a tremendously powerful thing. It has put a man on the moon and a toaster in every kitchen. Yet it is not quite as logical and dependable as we like to think, as we see in these examples. Is your judgement being affected by things you are unaware of?

One definition of wisdom is a working understanding of human imperfections. Today, a growing body of science, crossing many fields, is beginning to identify a taxonomy of these imperfections, known as cognitive biases, and, as such, provide a framework for wisdom.

Let us apply this directly to negotiations. Research has shown that if the discussion is framed in terms of profit, more concessions will be made; less will be made if it is about costs.

So, are you negotiating:

- on a potential profit or reduced costs?
- down from their requested price or up from your suggested figure?
- against your current salary or against the higher salary of the new position?

The answer to these questions will affect the result you get.

Similarly, our judgement will be impacted by anchors. An anchor is an opening figure which sub-consciously affects all ensuing judgements (so named because subsequent figures are connected to it like an anchor). For example, in one study, estate agents were shown a property and its list price and then asked to make their own independent valuation. Their results were significantly impacted by the published list price, even though 81% of the valuers said it was *not* part of their calculations.

So whoever opens the bidding, impacts the end point. Conclusion? You lead with the figures! And what if they get there first, how do you counter? One method is to mention a figure equally far in the other direction. Alternatively, you can talk about interests and objective standards and from there calculate a figure more impartial. If you use different measurement systems you can help scramble its effect on your brain.

Judgement audit

93% of drivers think they are better than average and it is a well-known fact that all men think they are better than average at sex. Of course, these beliefs cannot be true; everybody cannot be better than average, by definition.

Interestingly, it has been found that exactly the same patterns hold in negotiation. We tend to think our figures are more accurate than the other party, our reasoning is better, our behaviour is more flexible and co-operative and our viewpoint is more realistic and fair.

And yet, this cannot, of course, be true either. Both sides of the negotiation cannot be more accurate than the other. One can, but not both.

Then we look for evidence to support our view and ignore evidence to the contrary. We check our judgements with friends or colleagues who have similar opinions and we agree on a group-think. We become more and more certain about the validity and fairness of our thinking and the inaccuracy and unfairness of theirs.

So, how can we be sure that our thinking is as logical as we would like it to be? You need to do a judgement audit.

Firstly, be honest, brutally and painfully honest. You do not have to be open about it with other people but for god's sake be truthful to yourself. Also:

- Double-check your figures and your stories from different angles or sources
- Ask what could be wrong about them?
- Ask what question, experiment or evidence could prove it correct or incorrect?
- Ask the opinions of others who are likely to disagree with you.

- Take into account the other party's perspective and see what answer you would come to from that viewpoint.
- Work on the assumption that these are your best guesses but they could be wrong and plan for that scenario.

Having done that, do the same for the other party. They may be influenced by something less logical too. If you can identify that, you may be able to point it out to them diplomatically or you can just adjust for it in your thinking.

Even geniuses are irrational

Even the very best of us make irrational decisions. Sir Isaac Newton was one of the greatest geniuses who ever lived, he discovered the laws of motion and invented calculus. He also held one of the highest posts in government finance, as Master of the Royal Mint, was a wealthy man and a successful investor.

He bought shares in the South Sea Company, a joint stock company that had the rights to trade with Spanish territories in South America. The stock did well. In fact, it did very well. Soon, though, it got out of hand and Newton saw the speculation could not last. Saying "I can calculate the movement of the stars but not the madness of men", he wisely cashed in his investments for a handsome profit.

The stock, however, continued to rise. And continued to rise further. Newton could not help but feel he was missing out! He was unable to resist and he bought back into the company. Sadly, his first prediction proved correct, the market topped out, the South Sea Bubble burst and he lost a fortune.

Even geniuses can be irrational. Why, even George Soros makes financial decisions depending on how much his back hurts.

Simon Horton

Getting in the right frame of mind

There is one further thing to consider in your preparation that is almost as important as all of the above. And that is getting in the right frame of mind.

Have you ever noticed that sometimes you are in the right state of mind and you can do absolutely anything? You make a killer presentation to the board, you close an amazing deal, you score a brilliant goal. Top sports performers draw on this, it is a key part of their preparation because they know how much it affects their performance.

There are many things you can do and we will come across several in the course of this book. They are personal, not all of them work for everyone and you will need to identify which works best for you. Whichever technique it is, take the time to use it.

Which mood is the right mood?

But which frame of mind is the "right" one?

Confidence is probably the most commonly required state but it may be something else that is necessary. Think of your emotions as a palette of colours and for each particular meeting you may need a different colour. In fact, for each meeting you may need a different blend of colours to get exactly the right shade.

What about charming? There is a theory that the deal goes to the most charming. It is probably true in many cases. I know of one tremendously successful estate agent who started her career at the beginning of a massive property crash. When estate agents' offices were closing one after another, she went from strength to strength. She works by charm. Buyers and sellers love dealing with her. They go away feeling they have a win, no matter what, and they refer her to others.

Confident, charming, motivated, inspiring, tough, unmessable with, friendly, focussed, energised, calm, thoughtful, alert. There is a whole spectrum of emotions and choose the right one for you at any given time. You do not have to be at the whim of your mood, you can be in charge.

Practise mentally

In sports and the performing arts, where you simply have to perform at your best, mental rehearsal is a standard part of the preparation. Athletes see themselves crossing the winning line first, dancers mentally rehearse their moves. Each time they do this, they reinforce the neurology involved in the action.

Even to the extent that it builds muscle. For patients coming out of a long coma, their muscles can be too weak to do a movement, so their rehabilitation starts with visualising it. Remarkably, this actually builds the strength of the muscle to the point where the patient can then practise physically.

There is an argument that practising in your head is more effective than practising in real life. In one study, they divided a team of basketball players into three groups. One group practised for half an hour running up to the hoop and scoring; the second group did not practise at all; the third group spent half an hour mentally practising. The third group improved the most. Why? Probably because in their mental rehearsal they never missed (well, you wouldn't, would you?!), so they never reinforced the neurology of missing.

Who do you need to be?

The nervous negotiator worries and asks "But what shall I say?"; a better question is "How shall I be?". Then what to say will follow naturally.

Sound strange? Sound hippy? Relax, you will not have to sit in the lotus position and go 'om' or sing Tibetan chants whilst fumbling with your prayer beads (though feel free to give it a try in your next negotiation).

Actually, it is the fundamental premise of the U.S. Army Leadership Manual. Hard-core enough for you? Their leadership model is based on the triad

- Be
- Know
- Do

of which, being comes first. It is about character and actions follow from character. Once you have established the way you would like to be, the behaviour follows and the results follow.

So how do you change how you are being? Well, beyond joining the U.S. Army, simply answering that question, "How do I want to be?" can make the shift. And the answer will come to you – unstoppable, inspired, charming – and can make all the difference just as you step into the negotiating room.

Or, alternatively, "Who do I want to be?". Maybe you want to be Sir Richard Branson or Bill Gates or Superman or The Dark Knight or whoever will be that character that you *know* would get the right outcome. Then begin negotiations and be that person!

CHAPTER 5: DEVELOP YOUR PLAN B

Be prepared to walk away

He who cares least, wins.

So goes the saying at any rate and there is an element of truth to it in a negotiation. Power is partly a function of your willingness to walk away. If you decide to walk away from the deal, and the other party still want it, they will come towards you.

So you must be prepared to walk away from any deal. Being ok with this option will increase your power in the deal enormously.

We have all been in the market place, haggling for that nice ethnic vase. The asking price is way too high and on bargaining only comes down slightly. Walk away from the shop and the price drops instantly.

A more modern example we are all familiar with is the mobile phone company that rarely gives concessions to their existing customers. However, as soon as the customer says they are leaving to go to another provider, they will be transferred to the "Leavers Department" which is authorised to give much greater discounts on the contract.

Start with no

A useful dictum is to start with no. Go into every negotiation thinking that it is perfectly ok if you do not reach an agreement.

Do not be seduced by the dollar signs of a great deal. The more you are mesmerised, the greater the power they have over you. Make no mistake, they will try to create this need in you, they will talk about all kinds of promises, big deals, long contracts. You start thinking about the new house you are going to buy as a result and then you are caught. They make changes to the deal (beyond their control, of course) and you make concession after concession because you are so desperate for it.

Being over-dependent on any one deal is potentially catastrophic.

The Lovable Company made bras and lingerie since 1926, employing nearly 3000 staff. According to Frank Garson, their President, Walmart "awarded us a contract, and in their wisdom, they changed the terms so dramatically that they really reneged." Ultimately, they did this because they could. Walmart needed The Lovable Company less than the other way round. That is why they can squeeze margins until they squeak. And then a bit further.

Garson added "When you lose a customer that size, they are irreplaceable." Shortly after, in its 72nd year of operations, Lovable closed.

How do you prevent this from happening to you?

Be prepared to walk away. You do not need that Walmart deal. You lived without them before, you can live without them now. Do not be seduced by the dollar signs or anything else, do not let yourself be hypnotised.

You do not need any deal. Your survival and your happiness do not depend on any particular deal. You can walk away from any deal and still live and be happy. Therein lies your power. If this requires you building your cash in the bank, do so. But, whatever it takes, always be ready to walk away.

Now, *from that point*, start your negotiation, you will get a much better result from here. JP Morgan once commissioned a pearl scarf-pin from a famous jeweller. The jeweller crafted it and sent it with a bill for $5000. Morgan sent him a box and a cheque for $4000 and a note saying "I like the pin but I do not like the price. If you will accept this cheque, please send back the box with the seal unbroken." The jeweller was furious and tore up the check and sent the messenger packing. He opened up the box to take back his pin and found inside a cheque for $5000!

Indeed, invite a 'no'

Actively invite a 'no'. Say "Feel free to say no to this, but this is what I will need from this deal. If that doesn't work for you, that's fine...".

This is different from an ultimatum but it works in a similar way. An ultimatum often gets its result because people do not want to risk losing something. The downside, however, is that it can annoy people and they may not see it as negotiating in good faith.

Declaring your deal-breakers and inviting a 'no' still has the effect of potentially removing an offer from the table (which is likely to draw the other party towards you) but it does so in a rapportful way and people are actually impressed by the honesty. They go away feeling they know exactly where they stand.

And then be ready to walk away. They may well say "Thanks, but no thanks". Fine. On the other hand, they may well say "Yes, we can do business with you".

Knowing when to walk away from the deal

How do you know when to walk away? There is a simple answer to this. It is to compare the deal to your Plan B.

Fisher and Ury, in "Getting to Yes", call this your BATNA, which stands for Best Alternative To Negotiated Agreement, and it is a critical concept in negotiating. It is the basis of much of the power within a negotiation.

The BATNA is effectively what you would do if the deal fell through. In that instance, what is your next best alternative? On other words, what is your Plan B?

For example, you are at the market and you see a lovely vase and they are asking £20. What is a good price to pay and, conversely, at what point should you walk away? Well, let us imagine you have seen an identical one in a shop and it has a price tag of £15. This is your BATNA, your Plan B – if the deal falls through, you would go to the shop. You now have a very clear point at which you should walk away – if they accept £14.99 or less, you have a good deal; if they demand £15.01 or more, walk away.

Importantly, it gives you a guideline based on solid, real-world alternatives rather than a gut-feel of what seems reasonable.

It is extremely valuable for you to know what your other options are. It gives you a better idea of a fair deal and gives you greater power. To calculate an accurate idea of your Plan B, take into account any costs involved, too. For example, switching supplier may incur start-up costs.

And in the real-world the alternative is not always as clear as in the example above. You may have to be more sophisticated and consider your WATNA too. WATNA stands for Worst Alternative To Negotiated Agreement.

So, let us say you are in a dispute and should the discussions break down the alternative is to go to court. And let us say should you win, they will have to pay you £5,000. This is your BATNA. However, what if you lose? It may be you have to *pay* costs of £2,000. This would be your WATNA.

To be even more sophisticated, you can put percentages against each scenario and this will give you an even better guide to your walk-away point. Since the alternatives are not always cut-and-dried, you may wish to have in mind trigger points at which you decide to call a halt in the deal and take time out to ponder.

Make sure your choice is a considered one. Do you have a naturally competitive nature and are quick to follow the route of litigation or force? Or are you a natural appeaser, quick to give in and stick with the status quo. These may both be valid Plan B's but make sure you are analytical in your decision and do not simply follow your natural automatic impulse.

Increase your power, cultivate your alternatives

It is one thing to know your Plan B, it is yet another to cultivate it. As Bazerman and Neale point out in their book "Negotiating Rationally", if you are in the market for a house, never fall in love with one, fall in love with three! If you fall for just one, your negotiation room will be severely compromised.

Take the time, as part of your negotiation preparation, to cultivate your alternatives. Doing so will increase your bargaining position significantly.

Talk to several suppliers at the same time. Build a portfolio of clients and a pipeline of future sales. Look at the alternatives to this negotiation and invest in them. That investment will pay off in *this* deal.

Knowing your alternatives is an absolutely critical step to achieving your best deal. The U.S. Navy Seals know that circumstances will never be exactly as you wish so they plan accordingly. They have a saying, "Two is one and one is nothing". You can't rely on the weather, have a Plan B.

At what point will they walk away?

Of course, it works the other way too. If they show signs of walking away from the deal, it will put pressure on you to make concessions. If they are simply not budging from their position and they are happy to sacrifice the agreement, it can seem that they hold the power in the relationship and you are the side that has to make the compromise.

If you know *their* alternatives, however, you may be able to call their bluff.

Often people walk away from a deal without fully thinking through the impact. So, again, it can be useful to do the thinking for them. A gentle reminder of the consequences of not coming to agreement may bring them back to the table in a more accommodating manner.

Again, be sure to look at the true cost of the alternative. They may threaten to move to a different supplier who is cheaper, but have they considered the switching costs? The quality issues? The learning curve?

The risks? The new personalities involved? The new processes involved? Do the thinking for them and it can increase your persuasion power.

Knowing their Plan B will also give you a good idea of the most you are likely to be able to achieve from the deal. If you sell at one penny less, you probably have a sale; one penny more and you do not.

Their appetite for risk is important here, too. If the alternative is to go to court, say, there is an element of chance whether they win or not. Do they feel bullish about it or are they risk-averse? This is part of the equation.

Do the same for all the key players

Remember, negotiations are rarely one-on-one situations.

And in the same way that we found leverage from identifying all the key players involved and recognising the bigger picture interests of each, we can do the same with their Plan B's.

For each key player, step into their shoes and ask yourself what would they do if this deal were to fall through and, therefore, in what way is this deal beneficial for them.

This will give very useful information regarding how to influence them to support the deal.

Warn them before you walk away

Developing your Plan B is very much part of the Strong Win-Win system. It strengthens your hand to make sure you achieve your best deal and at the same time it decreases the chances of them trying to take advantage of you. If they play a win-lose game, fine, just walk away.

If it gets to the point that you are about to walk away, warn them of this fact and, if the warning is credible, this may be what is required to break the deadlock.

As part of the warning, get back to basics. Remind them why everybody is there in the first place and what you are trying to achieve and what they are trying to achieve.

Tell them of your Plan B and if this is better than what they are offering, they will see that your threat to leave the table is credible.

At the same time, remind them of *their* Plan B. If what your offer is better than this, make it clear to them.

In other words, make it very easy for them to say "yes" to the deal and give them one more chance to do so.

And let them know the consequences of the breakdown in talks. It may be that you will still be open to discussions should they ever change their mind, in which case let them know of the conditions for this to happen. On the other hand, if it means you signing a deal with another party and so this is Last-Chance Saloon, let them know of that too.

 Action points

Be prepared to walk away from this deal. Be prepared to walk away from *any* deal. Ask yourself:

▸ What is my Plan B?
▸ What is my WATNA, the worst-case scenario if the deal collapses?
▸ How can I cultivate more alternatives and make them more appealing?
▸ What is their Plan B and WATNA?

CHAPTER 6: ESTABLISH HIGH CREDIBILITY AND HIGH RAPPORT

Ok, so you have prepared and you have developed your Plan B. Now, roll your sleeves up, you are going to negotiate.

6.1 RAPPORT

Rapport is not essential to a negotiation, you are not there to win friends.

However, think about it: the deal is much more likely to be successful if you *are* friends. Friends are much more likely to help you achieve your win, friends are much less likely to deceive you or get their win at your expense.

Robert Cialdini, Professor Emeritus at Arizona State University, has done extensive research into the world of influence and documented his findings in the book, "Influence: The Psychology of Persuasion". He found six key rules of influencing and one of them is getting the other person to like you.

I am not saying become best friends with your counterparty. But I am saying that you will get a better deal if they like you. One study quoted by Cialdini (to be fair, a study of the bleedin' obvious) showed that waitresses that smiled increased their average tip from $9 to $22. So if your negotiating counterparty likes you, you will probably a get a better deal.

And the personal connection also proves very useful in the tricky moments of the discussions. When you come across a sticking point or when you find yourself apologising that, for reasons beyond your control, you have not been able to deliver your side of the bargain, it is the relationship that will get you through.

Ending the Cold War with a smile

"My name is Ron, can I call you Mikhail?". With that sentence, the course of world history changed.

Negotiations between the United States and the Soviet Union had been proceeding for decades at a glacial rate – two deadly

---

enemies with thousands of nuclear weapons aimed at each other, two deadly enemies who neither understood, liked or trusted the other.

Then one day, Ronald Reagan, in his first summit with Mikhail Gorbachev, saw the meeting was not going well and he suggested starting again. He put out his hand and introduced himself and asked if they could talk on first name terms. At that point, the Cold War ended.

Connecting at a personal level

Informality is a key element of building rapport, it transforms the situation from a transaction to a conversation. Unexpected informality, especially, can be a powerful ice-breaker because it enables people to relax in a situation which they may otherwise have experienced as stressful.

Introducing yourself informally and starting the meeting with small-talk will relax the other person from the outset. Indeed, choosing to hold the discussions in an informal context such as a coffee shop or at a sports event will make it natural to behave this way. Face-to-face is far better than email or letter, arguments conducted at a distance are often resolved quickly when the two parties meet in person. Humour is also very powerful in building the connection.

Needless to say, it can be taken too far. Some people are more comfortable with formal procedures so it is important to gauge the other person and the requirements of the situation. But as a broad rule of thumb, informality will produce a lighter atmosphere which most people will appreciate.

Anything that brings the conversation to a more human level is going to help the rapport. Talk about your family, ask them about theirs, talk about your holiday, empathise with their troubles in the traffic on the way to the meeting. The one thing we all have in common is we are human (if you are negotiating with anything else, that is beyond the scope of this book) and connecting at the human level is immensely powerful.

Being self-deprecating can help rapport. It shows you are not too self-important. Indeed, sometimes making a mistake or being a little clumsy can help as well. It can show your human side and it can help them feel more comfortable. People are often stressed about the expectations of their behaviour or performance and anything that communicates to them that there are no such expectations will help them feel more comfortable and will give them less need to be defensive.

Become "one of us"

According to Cialdini, people like people like them. We like and are more likely to respond to people who are like us: people who dress like us, who have similar backgrounds, who hold the same interests and hobbies as us, who hold the same political views, who are the same age, who have the same accents, the same behaviours and the same habits.

There is always some overlap between yourself and them and if you find it you will build a strong connection. I am from Essex and if I ever meet another person who is brave enough to admit they are from Essex, I will mention it and we will connect. What if I meet a Scotsman? I will point out that Robert the Bruce (the king who led Scotland successfully in its war of independence against England) was born in Essex! Instantly, we become brothers-in-arms! There is always an overlap to be found.

Mrs Thatcher famously liked to work with people who were "one of us", she valued this more than ability or experience. The more you can establish a commonality, the more you will become "one of us" and the deeper the rapport and trust will become.

Of course, it is important not to try *too* hard to become one of them, it can be excruciating when you see a salesman get it wrong!

Peas in a pod

The power of being "one of us" was illustrated in the negotiations that took place between the three major UK political parties after the hung election of 2010. The natural coalition would be between the Liberal Democrats and the Labour Party but apparently there was absolutely no affinity between their leaders, Nick Clegg and Gordon Brown.

In contrast, despite being natural political adversaries, Clegg and David Cameron, the leader of the Conservative Party, formed a very strong connection instantly. It became very clear that each saw the other as "one of us". They had very similar family backgrounds, they had gone to similar schools and to similar universities. Their lives within and outside of politics seemed to have more in common than not. They even looked similar – in their first press conference after sealing the deal, they looked like identical twins! They wore exactly the same suit and similar shirt and tie. They are exactly the same height and weight and even haircut and shape of face. Their voices sounded the same and they stood with the same posture and used the same gestures.

An unlikely coalition was formed thanks to each seeing the other as "one of us".

Create a "we" situation

Negotiations are often conducted in a "them against us" manner as the two parties sit across each other from the table. This starting point leads to stalemates and win-lose solutions.

You can change the dynamic by shifting the emphasis to the shared nature of the challenge and using "we" language. "The problem that we're facing together here ..." puts you both on the same side of the table.

You can even make this more tangible by sitting side by side instead of the more traditional approach of sitting across the table from each other. If the meeting did not start this way, write something on a flipchart or whiteboard, sit back down beside your counterparty, so you are both now alongside each other, sitting in the same direction, looking at whiteboard.

Create a "them and us" situation

Creating a common enemy can be an even more powerful way of strengthening the relationship. This can be a third party (eg, "We don't want to get the lawyers involved") or, of course, it could be the problem faced. It does not have to be a specific human being.

In 1954, Muzafer Sherif conducted a series of experiments at a summer camp in Robbers Cave State Park in Oklahoma. Firstly, boys were put into two different residence cabins. Each cabin was given a different team name and they engaged in competitive "them and us" games against each other. This rapidly led to hostilities between the teams until it was decided it was unsafe to continue the games any further.

He then introduced a different set of challenges where the teams had to co-operate to achieve common goals. It became a new "them and us" where the "us" was now both teams working together, and the "them" was the external challenge they faced (eg, the breakdown of the truck that brought food to the camp, a broken pipeline that brought the water).

As a result, people had to pull together and long-lasting friendships were formed between people who had previously been enemies.

Make them feel good about themselves

Showing that you appreciate the other person in a sincere fashion is very important for rapport. Nothing will kill rapport quicker than under-appreciating someone or disrespecting them.

Really listen to their point of view and acknowledge it. You do not have to agree with it but acknowledgement is very powerful. If you do disagree, you will get more success if you start by saying "I hear your point of view and I understand how important it is to you that... If I were in your position, I am quite sure I would feel exactly the same."

This is especially true if there is an emotion involved. The emotional content of a message is often more important than the factual content so, if it is appropriate, acknowledge this.

People like people who make them feel good so take the time to ask about them, talk about their interests and hobbies and other subjects you know will make them feel good. Enquire about their children or their achievements or their holidays. Look for something to compliment them on or ask their opinion on a subject.

Just how powerful this is was demonstrated by Jennifer Chatman, Professor in psychology at Berkeley, who found that flattery of your boss and making them feel good increased your chances of promotion. She decided to research this further, looking for the limit, the point beyond which smooth talking became obsequious and actually off-putting. Her conclusion was that this limit may exist but she could not find it in the data.

Another very powerful way of building rapport is to do them a favour. Show them that it is important to you that they get their win. Notice things they could get that they had not noticed themselves and then help them get it. And be fair in your own demands.

They also like us if we are linked with positive associations. We do not even have to cause these things, a mere association has an impact. Bring good news and, whether we caused it or not, we will be liked. Bring bad news and we will be disliked. So bring good news. Manage your surroundings and arrange the meeting at a nice or interesting venue. Take them to lunch at a good restaurant. They will unconsciously link these good feelings to you.

All of these things will make them feel good about themselves and if you can do that, you are on to a winner. They will trust you and they will repay that trust. They will be happy to help you get your win and they will be less likely to take advantage of you

What happens when you do not look for rapport

We started this section by saying that rapport was not essential. Let us look at an example where neither party considered rapport essential and the tragic consequences that followed.

George Mitchell, the U.S. Senator who chaired the Northern Ireland peace processes describes a visit by Bill Clinton to Northern Ireland to help give momentum to the peace process. He held consecutive half-hour meetings with Gerry Adams and with Ian Paisley. Now you may have thought an intelligent strategy would be to use this meeting to bring the President of the United States on your side and that building rapport would be a key part of this strategy.

Wrong. According to Mitchell, present at both meetings, Adams and Paisley each spent the whole half hour talking continuously at Clinton about their side of the story, without a single pleasantry or a single question of the President's views or feelings. In each case, Clinton did not "say anything other than 'Hello' and 'Goodbye'."

Such woeful negotiating skills. Persuasion through ranting is rarely successful. No wonder the decades of stalemate with neither side achieving their goals, instead, thousands dying in such a tragic and avoidable period in the country's history.

Limits to rapport

Now, remember, if you want friends, join a social club. You are at the negotiating table to get a deal. Rapport is key to this but it is not worth sacrificing the deal for sake of the relationship.

When Eastman Kodak outsourced their data centre operations to IBM, the negotiators on both sides wanted the very best deal they could get for their organisation and, at the same time, wanted a strong relationship between the two companies because they knew the success of the venture depended on that.

So they drew up two lists: one that related to the terms and conditions of the deal and one that was associated with the relationship. It was agreed that any problems on one list could not be resolved by a concession on the other.

Their relationship became almost an industry benchmark.

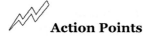 **Action Points**

Key to a successful negotiation is building a good relationship between the negotiators. There are many ways to build rapport:

▸ Be informal, smile, be friendly, help them relax
▸ Do small talk at the beginning of the meeting
▸ Connect at a human level
▸ Relate to them in such a way that helps them feel good about themselves
▸ Find an overlap in your background or hobbies or interest and show that you are 'one of us'.

6.2 CREDIBILITY

As important as it is to establish rapport at the beginning of the negotiation, it is equally important to establish credibility. High credibility will make you more influential, will show you can deliver on your promises and will deter others from bullying you.

Your credibility derives from a number of sources such as your position, your track record and your expertise. The stars or stripes on your shoulder may be visible to your counterparty but, if they are not, it is worth establishing your credentials during the introductions ("Just to give you a bit of background about myself, I ..."). Do not be too arrogant, but do not be too modest either.

You will want to highlight your experience in the particular field by your ease with the process and any jargon. Showing you are "one of them" is as important for credibility as it is for rapport. Industries where parties negotiate regularly over a prolonged period of time evolve a style together and you will want to show familiarity with this style. Consider the negotiations that take place between cinema chains and film distributors. With each new film, they meet to discuss terms which vary very little. They both work from the same figures, from the same spreadsheets, the same 'rules'. Their training will have consisted of case studies of real-life negotiations from previous years. They know each other, there is an industry culture. They have done it so many times, they 'know' what the deal is going to be even before they meet. In such a room, your credibility will depend on how much you know these things.

Credibility is also boosted, quite simply, by your input. Every time you suggest something that makes sense and every time your input leads to a successful outcome, you increase your credibility. So prepare. Make sure you know your field, make sure you know your case. Make sure you know the *other party's* case. This is where knowing your counterparty better than they do really pays off.

Demonstrate authority

If you had hearing problems, it is unlikely you would treat it by administering ear-drops up your backside.

In a funny (but rather worrying) example of unquestioning obedience to authority, a patient with an ear infection was prescribed ear drops to be administered to their right ear. The doctor wrote on the prescription, "Place in R ear". The nurse put the ear drops into the patient's anus. Neither nurse nor patient questioned it!

This story is recounted by Cialdini who says we will believe and follow the directions of someone we perceive to be an expert or an authority, even if what they tell us goes against our interests or own judgements.

In one study, a researcher, identifying himself as a doctor, instructed a nurse (22 separate nurses in the experiment altogether) to administer a particular medication to a patient. The medication was for an unauthorised drug and the dosage was at a dangerous level. Furthermore, the instruction was given over the phone, contrary to hospital policy, and by somebody who the nurse had never met before but simply identified himself as a doctor. 95% of the nurses complied unhesitatingly.

The importance of looking important

So human beings have a natural tendency to follow authority even if they only have the trappings of authority.

If someone wears a uniform, their requests of or orders to strangers will be a lot more successful. This can also be true if they are simply wearing a suit. In an experiment conducted in Texas, a man violated the law by crossing a road against the street-lights and the experiment was to see how many people would follow him. Half the time the experiment was conducted he wore a suit and tie, half the time he wore shirt and trousers. Three and a half times as many people followed him when he wore the suit as when he dressed more casually.

Frank Abagnale, the con-man whose story was played by Leonardo DiCaprio in the Spielberg film "Catch Me If You Can", flew over a million miles with Pan-Am for free, staying at hotels with all food and lodging billed to the airline. This despite the fact that he did not work for them! He did, however, wear a pilot's uniform and this enabled him to fool all involved.

I am not suggesting you wear a pilot's uniform in your next negotiation. However, if you want to increase your credibility, one way of doing this is to wear the trappings of authority. Wear a smart suit and tie. Carry an impressive bag. Use an expensive pen and notepad or a top-of-the-range computer. Meet at a well-to-do restaurant or the lobby of a 5-star hotel. What are the trappings of authority in your field? Wear them to create a quiet air of authority.

Increase your credibility by looking confident

According to Deborah Tannen, CEO's have to make a decision in 5 minutes on something a team has spent five months investigating. Often, they make their decision on how confidently the argument is put.

This is almost certainly true and, at the same time, it is quite amazing. Come up with a bunch of rubbish and present it confidently, you will get it through. On the other hand, do careful research and consider lots of risk and probabilities, and present it with concomitant uncertainty, it will get chucked out.

So if you want to put your argument across successfully, act and speak confidently.

Speak confidently

When you speak, use words that imply confidence and talk in a strong voice.

Project your voice, talk loudly (but not too loudly) and slowly (but not too slowly). Articulate each letter clearly and let your voice resonate, deeper voices tend to come across more confident than higher ones.

Don't use words like 'might', 'maybe', 'perhaps', hopefully', 'probably', 'possibly', 'I think', 'try', 'if' and other such words that undermine the listener's belief you know what you are talking about.

Instead, use words that imply confidence like 'you will', 'I am going to', 'clearly', 'the obvious conclusion', 'therefore', 'when' and similar words.

The word 'because' is an interesting one. Harvard social psychologist Ellen Langer conducted a famous experiment where she studied people's ability to jump the queue for the photocopying machine. In the first instance, the individual asked "Excuse me, I have 5 pages. May I use the Xerox machine?"; in the second, they asked "Excuse me, I have 5 pages. May I use the Xerox machine because I'm in a rush?"; and in the third, "Excuse me, I have 5 pages. May I use the Xerox machine because I have to make copies?"

The study found a 60% success rate in the first instance, where there was no reason given, simply a request made. It found a 94% success rate when a good reason was given, that the individual was in a rush. However, the interesting finding was that they found a 93% success rate when the individual said "because I have to make copies" – an almost identical success rate even though the reason was given was nonsensical (like, the others weren't there to make photocopies?!).

In the follow-up to this experiment, they repeated the same situation with the only difference being that the requester had to make 20 photocopies. This was a much bigger favour to ask than a quick 5 copies and in this set-up the word 'because' lost its magic. In this instance, the success rate was 24% with no reason, 42% with a good reason and back to 24% with a nonsensical reason.

So back up your arguments with a reason and use the word 'because'. The bigger the ask, the more plausible the reason should be.

Why? Because!

How Much Is A Million Pounds Worth?

In 1994, the English dance band, the KLF, burnt a million pounds then tried to sell the ashes as a work of art. How much did they get for them?

Jimmy Cauty and Bill Drummond had been successful in the music industry, in different guises, for several years. As the KLF, despite an anti-establishment philosophy, they became the biggest selling singles act across the world in 1991.

Amongst other controversial episodes, they set up the K Foundation art award. This was in response to the Turner Prize, the British arts prize of £40,000 awarded to the best artist each year. The K Foundation prize, announced on the same day as the Turner Prize, was also for £40,000 and given to the *worst* artist of the year. Coincidentally, it was given to the same artist.

They decided to use the proceeds from their hit records to support struggling artists. But they changed their minds when, as Drummond said, "we realised that struggling artists are meant to struggle, that's the whole point". So, in 1994, they chose to burn the money instead. In a boathouse on Jura, an island off Scotland, they fed a million pounds in £50 notes into a fire.

They kept the ashes and later, probably feeling a little silly about what they had done, took them around various art galleries in London and asked if they would sell them as a work of art.

Each gallery refused. The ashes, it turned out, were worth nothing.

Now, the galleries refused for this reason: the KLF asked was it a work of art. In doing so, they completely undermined the credibility of their argument. Art does not ask for permission to exist.

If, instead, they had *declared* it a work of art, its status would not have been disputed and they would have got a deal.

In contrast to the KLF's uncharacteristic self-doubt, we will come across another artist, later in the book, who was confident in his declaration, and changed the course of art history.

Use confident body language to boost your credibility

If communication is core to negotiation, non-verbal communication is a massive part of this. Famously, Albert Mehrabian, Professor Emeritus of Psychology at UCLA, suggested that in communications about emotions, *only 7%* of the meaning came from the words themselves, 38% came from tone of voice and 55% from visual cues such as facial expression and other body language. (In one source, not to be named, I saw this as 7%, 35% and 55%. Obviously, the other 3% came from their ability in maths!).

Whether or not we agree with the precise figures, it is clear non-verbal communication is very important. If you were to ask me do I like tomatoes, I could reply "yeah!" with gusto and my eyes lighting up, or I could reply "yeah" in a low-energy kind of way and with a snort at the end. The first would imply I love them, the second I hate them. Exactly the same verbal content, polar-opposite meanings.

So if we can become fluent in this language, it can help us communicate much better.

If you use confident body language, two things happen. The first, strangely, is that you actually start to feel confident. The emotion and the physiology are linked in the brain and the link is two-way. If you feel confident, you will stand and move in a particular manner. Conversely, if you stand and move in that manner, the confidence will follow. Studies have shown a measurable rise in testosterone levels when an individual makes a "power pose".

The second thing that happens is the other party will respond to you *as though you were* confident. You project greater credibility and they respond accordingly. After all, they can only see what is on the outside. Inside, you may be feeling terrible and thinking it is a disaster but if you look confident, they will not know. So they will respond to you as though you are confident and this, in turn, will make you actually feel more confident.

Most professional sports and entertainment stars use this. We think they are perfectly at home performing in front of large crowds but in actual fact they are often very nervous before events. At the Live 8 concert in Hyde Park in the summer of 2005, David Beckham introduced Robbie Williams to the crowd. Afterwards, in an interview, Williams described how incredibly nervous he had been before going on stage but he looked over and saw that Beckham was even more nervous! This, he said, made him feel better! Here were two of the most successful and experienced performers in the world and both were completely nervous. And yet, despite this, when they walked on stage, they both looked totally confident and that was what the crowd saw. The crowd cheered and the performers immediately found their confidence.

So what is confident body language? Well, before I answer that, here is a question for you. We can tell if someone is confident often before they speak. We can see two people, one confident and one not so, and even before they open their mouth we can usually tell which one is the more self-assured. So, given they have not yet spoken and given we cannot mind read, how can we tell that one person is confident and the other is not?

Think of someone you know who projects self-assuredness. Ask yourself what is it that they are doing, at the level of body language, that communicates that? Then do those things yourself. Conversely, next time you see someone who seems lacking in confidence, ask yourself what is it that they are doing that communicates that? Then make sure you do not do those things yourself.

For most people, confident body language is

- stand tall
- shoulders back and head up
- strong gestures
- intentional movements

- walking purposefully
- strong handshake
- looking people in the eye
- being comfortable taking up space
- hand gestures with the palms facing down
- steepling – placing the hands together in front of the face, with the fingertips touching.

Indeed, in the wise words of Val Doonican's mum, "Walk tall and look the world right in the eye." And with his cardigans and rocking-chair, who could doubt Val Doonican's credibility!

Add credibility with the written word

Despite the fact that writing is a modern invention, in evolutionary terms, we tend to give more credence to something if it is written down. If we hear a story or purported fact, that is one thing. If we read about it, that is something else, we give it more legitimacy. You can use this to your advantage.

Have written reports and spreadsheets printed that you can refer to frequently in your discussion. Refer to them as though they are absolute truth and it is harder for the other party to counter or dismiss.

In fact, the more 'solid' the document, the more persuasive. Present it in a bound document, like a book, and it will have greater authority still.

 **Action points**

Your credibility is equally as important as rapport and you need to establish this early on too. You can do this by:

▸ Demonstrating your proven track record
▸ Preparing thoroughly and showing your knowledge of the subject at hand and developing workable solutions
▸ Talking confidently and using confident body language
▸ Being assertive (as opposed to passive or aggressive) in response to intimidation.

6.3 RAPPORT VS CREDIBILITY

Of course, it is not a question of doing one or the other; successful negotiators do both.

It is about getting the right balance. At any given point, you want to consider which one you need to focus on. If you have spent too much time proving you are a tough cookie, now might be the time to relax and smile a bit. Alternatively, if you have spent a while chit-chatting and exchanging pleasantries, now might be the time you roll your sleeves up and get down to some serious work.

Consider it like plate spinning. You want to get both plates spinning well. But at any one point it may be one plate that needs a little extra attention.

Which should you start with? Of course, that depends. It depends upon the demands of the particular meeting and anything you know about the counterparty. It also depends very much on you and what is your natural tendency. If your natural tendency is to be a pleaser, then perhaps you should focus a little more on your credibility at the beginning. Alternatively, if you tend to come across sternly, perhaps you should start the meetings asking them about their weekend.

Are you a dog or a cat?

Michael Grinder has studied the behavioural features of charismatic people and has written about them in his excellent book, The Elusive Obvious. He puts a lot of it down to finding the right balance between credibility and rapport.

He talks of two types of people: dogs and cats. Dogs think: "This person brings me food every day and lets me sleep in their home? Wow, they must be a god." Cats think: "This person brings me food every day and lets me sleep in their home? Wow, *I* must be a god."

Dogs are the pleasers, they are dependent and like to be around other people, they reference themselves in terms of other people. For dogs, the important thing is that everyone feels good about themselves. These people are high on rapport.

Cats are independent, they define their own reality. For cats, it is not about feeling good, it is about results. They do not mind hurting people's feelings as long as the job gets done well. These people are high on credibility.

If you are naturally a dog, you may consider being a little more cat-like in your dealings. If you are naturally a cat, you may consider being a little more dog-like.

Take a second to think about yourself how others see you. Would people naturally come to you for a chat or are they a little scared of you? On the other hand, if a tough job needed doing would they turn to you? Or would they give it to someone else?

Knowing how others see you in this respect can give you an idea of where you need to focus to build more charisma. Of course, it is impossible to really see yourself in the same way others do so it is worth seeking external feedback on this. Hmm, scary!

The body language of cats and dogs

Grinder also sees body language as crucial in whether we come across as credible or approachable. He breaks it down as follows:

	Rapportful	Credible
Voice:	Voice rhythmic but ends upwards	Voice flat but ends downwards
Pace and energy:	Tends to talk quickly and excitedly	Talk more slowly, pause more
Hand:	Gesturing hand, palm up	Firm hand, pointing down
Gestures:	Animated	Very few
Head:	Lots of nodding	Still head, starting up finishing down
Facial expression:	Smiling and animated	No facial expression
Body posture:	Joints flexible, loose	Joints locked, stiff, leaning forward.

Get the balance. If you need to boost the rapport – loosen up and do more of the things on the left-hand column. If you want to raise your credibility – toughen up and do more of the things on the right.

Action points

Rapport and credibility are not mutually exclusive but you may want to give more emphasis to one than the other at different times.

▸ Notice your natural leaning – is it to be friendly or are you more focussed on delivery?
▸ At any point in the negotiation, be aware if you need to give more attention to the rapport or to your credibility.

6.4 INCREASING YOUR POWER

To the lion, his share

In Aesop's fable, a lion goes hunting with a sheep, a cow and a nanny goat (I know, not a very plausible storyline but stay with me, the man's got a good track record). They pull down a large stag and they get ready to divide out the spoils.

The lion says, "Let's be fair about this. We'll divide the catch into four equal parts. I will get the first part because I helped kill it. Now, since I am the King of the Jungle I should get the second part, too. The third part is mine because I am the strongest. And if anyone wants the last part, they can fight me for it."

Such is power.

Power is a critical aspect of the Strong Win-Win method. They are unlikely to bully you if they see an army behind you. Indeed, the larger your army, the greater their propensity for win-win. Surprisingly.

But it is a misunderstood concept so we will spend time to look at its nature and how you can increase it and use it wisely

Power is the ability to get your way with or without the other party's agreement and irrespective of natural fairness. It is not advisable to use force in such a manner. The reason? It is that principle of 'Never Be Rude To The Waiter'. You may force them to sign something but they sure as hell ain't going to implement it the way you would like them to.

However, where power may be useful is in response to theirs. If they are trying to force you to give way, you may have to apply force in return. Or, better, your *show* of force can deter any temptation they may have had, without actually putting it to use. If you abide by Roosevelt's dictum of "Speak softly and carry a big stick", you may have to make that stick visible in order to avoid using it.

Brute physical force

At its most primitive, power is down to brute physical force.

In stone-age days, if you were stronger than your neighbour, you won most arguments. In Viking days, if you had a bigger army, you could plunder the goods and wealth of the nearby lands.

In some instances, it has not progressed very far. If you have ever travelled on the Indian sub-continent, you will know the laws of the road there are very simple. There is only one rule: "If it is bigger than you, give way". You can drive wherever you like and in any direction you like but pedestrians give way to cyclists, cyclists give way to motorbikes, motorbikes give way to cars, cars give way to lorries. There is only one exception: all vehicles give way to the cow.

That one exception apart, it is all about size and strength.

It can seem that way too in your negotiation. Your boss is telling you to work late and there seems no alternative. Your customer, an industry giant, has such a wide reach in the marketplace that you have to accept their unreasonably tough terms. Your ex-partner is taking you to the cleaners and they have the law on their side.

They get their way because of sheer brute force.

And yet, as we shall see, brute force is just one very small part of the power equation.

What if they are more powerful than you?

When threatened with danger, our natural instincts kick in and our fight/flight/freeze response takes over. Fair enough if being chased by a bear but in a negotiation the same wiring gets activated and it is less appropriate. The problem is that it shuts down our rational brain and we no longer see the situation for what it is.

When I run negotiations courses, my students often ask what you can do when the other party is much stronger than you.

This question pre-supposes a lot. It pre-supposes:

- that they really are stronger and not bluffing
- that they are willing to actively use that power
- that it will be necessarily to your disadvantage
- that a win-win does not exist which is an attractive solution to them compared to their alternatives
- that they do not see *you* as the powerful one
- that there is only the one basis of power and that is the one in which they are stronger.

It only requires one of these to be a misconception and the issue is resolved.

In actual fact, it is quite possible that *every single one* of these assumptions is wrong. It is just we do not see it that way because our fight/flight/freeze response blinds us to the reality.

Simon Horton

Let us take the last one first.

French and Raven's Five Bases of Power

So if not physical force, what are the other sources of power?

In 1959, French & Raven produced what has become a classic study of social psychology and identified five bases for power, to which they later added a sixth.

The first they labelled **Legitimate Power** (legitimate, as in compliance with the law and accepted authority). This is power that lies with an individual because of their status or position. For example, they are your boss or they are a policeman or the building regulations department in the council or they are the person in charge of the stationery cupboard and you are after a new stapler.

Secondly, they identify **Referent Power** as another source (referent as in that which is referred to). Their usage of the term relates to charm or charisma or the ability to persuade and attract loyalty. Whereas legitimate power is based on a nominal status, this is based on personal qualities and interpersonal skills.

Their third source of power is **Expert Power**, that is the power that comes from skills and knowledge in a particular field or process. In a legal dispute, a lawyer will get their power, to a large degree, from their knowledge of the law and their ability to apply it to the given situation. In a business negotiation, an individual may well hold power because of their ability to make a business success out of a proposition or because of their operational knowledge of what is practically feasible and what is not. Either instance would be examples of expert power.

Information Power is a variation on Expert Power that French and Raven added later. It is the power that comes from access to useful information, whether that person is an expert or not. Knowing what is going on in the market, or knowing the thinking of the Chief Executive Officer, or knowing that the Council building regulations are about to change, would all be instances of information lending power to the person who holds it.

Coercive Power is the ability to punish or inflict negative consequences on the other person, a power that is based on fear. And its converse is **Reward Power** which is the ability to bestow benefits on the other person.

Other sources of power

There are other sources of power beyond those identified by French and Raven.

• The power of the idea

The power of the idea is an immense force. Whether the idea is a religion or a nation or a value such as freedom, people have been willing to forfeit their lives for ideas. That is powerful. Would anyone in your negotiating team be willing to lay down their lives for your current deal? I thought not!

So increase your power in a negotiation by focussing the other party on an inspiring concept; as George Mitchell did in Northern Ireland, constantly reminding the negotiators of the historic nature of the process they were involved in.

• The ability to persuade

Your ability to persuade is a key source of power.

So, want to increase your power? Listen! Listen, because they will tell you exactly how to persuade them. Let them do the talking and as they do they will tell you how to increase your power.

Listen in between the lines and they will tell you of their drivers. Put the deal in those terms. Show them the benefit of doing the deal and the costs to them of not doing it and, if it really is of value to them, they should come around. If not, you simply have not shown them sufficient value.

• Access to resources

Access to other resources will increase your power. If the definition of power is impact in the world, any resource that will help increase that impact will increase your power. This can be money, numbers of people, influential people or experts, machinery, computing power, institutions, any number of things.

If that access is unique, or at least scarce, this will increase your power but if other people have the same resources, your power is diminished.

Take AOL, in the 1990's they were extremely powerful because they had built a "walled garden", many prime sites on the internet could only be accessed through their system. They became so powerful they were able to buy out Time Warner in one of the greatest ever business deals. However, as soon as the rest of the World Wide Web offered just as much utility, and then more, without having to pay AOL's membership fee, AOL lost the basis of its power.

And it is not just access to resources, of course, it is your ability to co-ordinate them and bring them to bear. So take Google, then, part of the very reason for AOL's downfall. Where does *their* power come from? It actually comes from their ability to leverage the rest of the internet. Without the internet, Google's search algorithms would be nothing. But without Google, the internet would be less of a resource. And as soon as a better algorithm comes along, that leverages the internet even better, Google's power will decrease.

In this respect, your power in the negotiation is proportional to your power *outside* of the negotiation. So work to enhance your power in the world through your network or family or organisation.

If you are negotiating on behalf of an organisation, your power is a function of the power of the organisation *multiplied by your power within* the organisation. That is, the organisation may have many resources to bring to the deal but to what extent can you mobilise them? Similarly, with the other party. If they are not powerful within their organisation, their promises or threats are less likely to be followed through.

Therefore, to increase your power in the negotiation, use the skills you are learning in this book to increase your power in your organisation – you will be able to bring more of its weight to bear.

- **Brand and reputation**

Brand is a massive point of leverage which is why companies are so protective of it.

Charities punch above their weight because of this. Think of Amnesty International, one of the biggest brands in the world, yet with an annual income of just £44m (2009). Many profit-driven companies with the same level of global awareness would have revenues of a thousand times that.

Individuals have a brand too, it is their reputation. Consider Nelson Mandela, Gandhi, Jimmy Carter. They built a reputation that has a power in the world.

Much of Mandela's reputation was built whilst in jail. The bigger his reputation grew, the more his detainment became a source of power for him. This led to the strange situation when he and De Klerk were discussing his release – he wanted to stay in jail and De Klerk wanted him out!

You can increase your power by reputation around trust. This is a power source, people will honour it.

- **Creativity**

As we have seen, creativity is an essential element of negotiations and it can change the power balance significantly. It can enable you to come up with the win-win solution that will shift the balance in your favour. Or, in a situation where they are trying to muscle you into something that you do not want, it may give you a way to out-flank them.

The classic scenario of the power imbalance is the big retailer negotiating with its suppliers. And no retailer comes bigger or more powerful than Walmart so many are the stories of woe from suppliers who feel the muscle of Walmart. What is the best response?

According to Gib Carey, a partner at Bain & Co, who has studied successful and unsuccessful partnerships with the retail giant, the solution is to innovate. "You need to bring Walmart new products, products consumers need. Because with those, Walmart doesn't have benchmarks to drive you down in price. They don't have historical data, you don't have competitors, they haven't bid the products out to private-label makers. That's how you can have higher prices and higher margins."

Similarly, a few years back, McDonalds demanded all of their suppliers reduce their prices by 10%. They did this because they could, such was their power. Now their cup supplier, the Sweetheart Cup Company, at the same time found that *their* supplier were about to *increase* their prices so Sweetheart would be squeezed in the middle. So they arranged a meeting with all three parties present to find ways to deliver. The imaginative process improvements that came out of putting all heads together meant lower prices, higher volumes and higher quality for everyone.

So if the other party exerts its power on their key variable (eg, price), you will have to be creative to find other ways to combat this. If you stick to fighting on their terms, simply price, they will probably win the arm-wrestle because they are stronger than you. If they are stronger, you have to out-flank them. Be creative, increase the number of variables, find other ways to increase value. Assert your company's needs and turn their demands into a problem that both of you can solve together.

Creativity is, perhaps, the most important single source of power.

- **Willingness to walk away**

Power is a function of willingness to walk away. We have seen this in chapter 5, "Develop Your Plan B". If the other party senses your desperation for the deal, they are unlikely to make any concessions. On the other hand, if you do start to walk away, they will soon move towards you if they want the deal.

So always be sure that you can walk away. You do not need any deal. From that point, start your negotiation and you will get a much better result.

- **Choosing the framework**

Power is dependent on the frame of the negotiation. Change the frame and you change the power distribution.

If you have a piece of paper with some scribbles on it, what is that worth? Maybe nothing if you are in a war-zone or you are starving. Or maybe millions if it is a Picasso and you are in a New York auction house. Modigliani was a bohemian artist who died in poverty in 1920 at the age of 35 from tubercular meningitis. To survive, and to pay for his drug addiction, he would often swap works of his art for a meal in a restaurant. In 2010, one of his works was sold for £36m.

The KLF, we saw, asked the galleries what the deal was about – was it about a work of art or was it about a pile of ashes? The galleries chose the latter.

Marcel Duchamp, on the other hand, famously signed a urinal "R. Mutt" and declared it a work of art. In doing so, he set the framework for its valuation. Prior to this, it was simply a urinal, worth the same as any other you could buy from a discount bathroom store. Afterwards, it became an icon, voted in 2004 the most influential work of art of all time and, as such, worth millions. Unfortunately, it has been lost! Someone, somewhere, is unknowingly urinating on a fortune! Next time you go to the toilet, check for any writing on it. If it says "R. Mutt", you are in luck. If it says "Armitage Shanks", sorry.

What is the negotiation 'about'? The other person may say it's just a toilet, you may say its the work of a genius. Whatever it is 'about' will affect the price massively. You can *choose* what it is about. Is the deal about profit or about market share? Is it about short-term gain or long-term gain? Is it about risk? Is it about publicity? Is it about pride? Revenge?

Change the frame of the game and you change the power balance.

Choose your power source and use it appropriately

As the American proverb says, "A Smith & Wesson beats four aces". As we have seen, there are many power sources and you can choose the one that suits you best. **Do your SWOT analysis to identify the power that you do have and then ask where and how you could use it most effectively?**

When David took on Goliath, who had the greater power? Goliath, of course, he was famed for being such a strapping giant. But David was not stupid, he did not start wrestling with him, he would have been mincemeat. Instead, he changed the game and used a slingshot. He was a dead-eye with that and he did not have to get within reach of Goliath's great big hairy arms which would have pulled him to pieces. He changed the rules, hit him with a stone in between the eyes and knocked him cold.

In 1865, the Prussian statesman Bismarck challenged his political opponent, Dr Rudolf Virchow, to a duel and, in accordance with duel etiquette, Virchow was allowed to choose the weapons. Virchow would not have stood a chance using any traditional weapon so he chose sausages! One was fresh, the other infected with cholera, Bismarck could choose which he ate. Instead, he called off the duel.

Choosing the rules of the game is itself a rule encoded in duelling – the person who is challenged can choose the methodus pugnandi, or the weapons to be used. David chose a slingshot, Virchow chose sausage.

Choose the rules that will suit you best and redress any power imbalance.

Choose your weapons

In 2010, a concerted campaign from Greenpeace successfully persuaded Nestlé to stop sourcing their supplies from rainforest destruction. To do this, Greenpeace took on the combined might of Nestlé, Cargill and the palm oil industry.

Let us look at the power balance in this issue, using annual revenue as a measure:

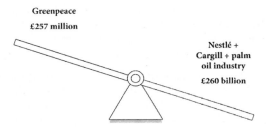

Greenpeace
£257 million

Nestlé +
Cargill + palm
oil industry
£260 billion

Hmm, Greenpeace did not seem to have much of a chance in this one!

On the other hand, Greenpeace had different weapons at its disposal. They had a brand and they were not afraid to use it. They had a track record of taking on big companies and winning so Nestlé and Cargill knew they were going to be in for a battle. Did they really have the stomach for a fight? After all, Nestlé also had a brand and they were keen to protect it.

Greenpeace had another power source too – a worldwide army of supporters. A worldwide army of supporters all driven by an idea – that saving the planet was more important than profits for a few. They were quite a motivated bunch.

Of course, these supporters had to be co-ordinated, they did not all work in Greenpeace HQ. However, if there was one capability that Greenpeace had that really made it such a force to reckon with it was its tremendous capacity for organising a coherent movement. Using a viral campaign, 1.5million clicked to watch their video, and social networks to organise the protests, they decided to focus their energies on a critical minority - Nestlé's shareholders. It all took place at the Annual General Meeting on April 15th in Lausanne. Protestors dressed as orang-utans demonstrated outside. Inside, they dropped

banners down from the ceiling asking Nestlé to give orang-utans a break, Kit Kat style. A fake Wi-Fi network was set up sending shareholders directly to www.greenpeace.org/kitkat as they logged on, where tweeting supporters let them know their feelings.

Greenpeace had billions of dollars lined up against them but, like David against Goliath, they chose to play a different game. They used brand, resources, an idea, co-ordination, credibility, humour, creativity and modern technology as their weapons of choice.

The result? On May 17th, Nestlé committed to identifying and excluding companies from its supply chain that own or manage 'high risk plantations or farms linked to deforestation'.

Do not buy into their power

Whichever power source, so much of it is based on *perception* and you do not need to buy into any particular perception.

If you are negotiating with Walmart, they may well think their size and market access will give them much more power in the deal than you. If they have already agreed an exclusive supplier relationship with you, they will be sure of this even more. But you do not have to buy into this. If you are ready to walk away, *they no longer have that power*.

Consider the bully who is challenged: if you do not buy into their power, they have none.

Conversely, how you present yourself and your side is important to how much they buy into your power. It is not about bluffing, it is about presenting your situation in the best possible to light to display your power. Like birds that ruff up their feathers to make them look bigger, it is just so it does *not* come to a fight. The comfortable display of power means it never has to be used.

Be prepared to use your power fairly

At the same time, you must be willing to *use* any power base you have otherwise it will not be credible. You may have a nuclear weapon, but are you going to use it? The law may be on your side, but will it be too much effort to impose? Your supplier may be breaking the contract but if they are based in China how will you enforce it?

Be prepared to use your power but use it as a last resort and make it easy for them to say yes at the same time as you make it hard for them to say no.

During the Cuban Missile Crisis, it was only because Kennedy demonstrated credibly that he was prepared to go to war that the Soviets backed down. But even as he did this, he kept another offer visible which allowed them a way out whilst still keeping face.

Use your power skilfully because otherwise it will prove counter-productive. If you exert power unnecessarily, they are very likely to use power in response and it will rapidly go downhill.

And use it fairly because otherwise, as we have seen, the other side will feel aggrieved and will look to hurt you in response, even if it hurts themselves in doing so.

How to set up your own cult and other top tips

Of course, there is another approach which is the Machiavellian school – this is not about using force but deceit; probably perfect for the mediaeval court when your aim was to maximise your wealth at others' expense, whilst avoiding being beheaded or other such unfortunate mishaps. A great intro to this school is Robert Greene's "48 Laws of Power" which includes such laws as:

- Get others to do the work for you but always take the credit
- Pose as a friend, work as a spy
- Crush your enemy totally
- Discover each man's thumbscrew

It is a great book and provides a lot of insight into human nature. Many of the laws even work but in the same way that "Nuke your enemies" would work too. If you nuked your enemies, they would certainly never bother you again but there may be fall out! And dealing with that fall out just may not be worth the effort.

Anyway, there are better ways - more successful, less risky. Even the mediaeval courts realised this and evolved into the "French" method of diplomacy which was based on honour and trust.

That said, Greene's book has several good things to be said about it. For example he gives you 5 easy steps to create a cult:

Step 1: Keep it vague, keep it simple

Step 2: Emphasise the visual and the sensual over the intellectual

Step 3: Borrow the forms of organised religion to structure the group

Step 4: Diagnose your source of income

Step 5: Set up an "us-versus-them" dynamic

There you are, now off you go and set up your own cult. Ok, it might not be as clear as an Ikea flat-pack instruction leaflet (Greene does give you a few more details) but think how much better your negotiations will be if you have a gang of bright-eyed fanatics behind you.

What to do in a hopeless case

Sometimes, unfortunately, you do find yourself in a situation where it really does seem a hopeless case. They are using force and they can. What to do then? Here are some possibilities beyond what we have just discussed:

- Prepare fully, you will be more likely to take advantage of anything that does come up.
- What are your strengths/weaknesses? Can you use your strengths to their full advantage? Can you turn your weaknesses into strengths?
- Build *big* rapport, they are less likely to be ruthless.
- Bluff as much as you can – ruff up your feathers!
- Get stuck in and see what evolves – maybe you will be pleasantly surprised.
- Take a risk; it is a hopeless case anyway, what is the worst that can happen?
- Maybe you can re-frame the outcome, see it in a different light so that the result is not so bad after all.
- Beat a polite retreat and fight the wars you *can* win.

Sometimes we have to take a hit. We cannot expect to win every battle in life. But, remember, it is not about winning the battle, it is about winning the war.

Action points

Skilful negotiators, like Greenpeace in the story above, know there are many dimensions to power.

▸ Do not take their power at face value
▸ Identify your own power sources and set the framework of the deal
▸ Build your power sources over time so they are there when you need them
▸ Be creative
▸ Be fearless and be willing to walk away.

CHAPTER 7: MOVE THEM TO WIN-WIN

7.1 TURN THEM INTO A SWORN-IN WIN-WIN FANATIC

This chapter is pivotal to the Strong Win-Win strategy. A common reason for not playing win-win is that it only works if the other person plays it too. And there is a truth in this. But it is not a reason for changing tactics, it just means you have to move their thinking to win-win. Which is often quite straight-forward.

Many people are naturally win-win and doing business with these will be pleasant, rapid and highly productive all-round. Some people are naturally win-lose, indeed some steadfastly so. That is fine, these are a minority and we will see ways of dealing with these later.

But the large majority dither somewhere in the middle and they will need a helping hand. It need not be difficult – if you really are offering them a good deal, and it is communicated to them clearly, why would they not?

In a way, the whole book is about moving the other party to win-win. If you have prepared thoroughly, thinking about it from their side and yours, if you have developed a strong Plan B and if you have established high credibility and high rapport, most people will be on your side already and will be working with you. Add in the creative problem-solving techniques of the next chapter and the checks and balances in chapter 9, and you have many, many strategies to help you.

Here we will look at some other powerful methods to shift their thinking in the way you want it to go. Whether through being the example of the behaviour you wish to see, channelling their self-interest or other means, you can enter the negotiation confident they will respond positively. Do not rely on hope they will be a nice person, do not cross your fingers that they will like you – do something about it and make them win-win.

So what exactly can we do to turn them into a sworn-in win-win fanatic with the t-shirt and the certificate to prove it?

Be the example of the behaviour you want to see

Ok, listen up, here is a secret of the universe. I am going to say it quietly, so move in closer to the book. If you want people to behave in a certain way, this is a trick that works. It is almost like a magic wand – wave the wand and they will be how you want them to be. It is tremendously powerful. Ok, here is the secret: the large majority of people respond in kind to your behaviour. Consequently:

If you are:	They will be:	The result:
Stubborn and refuse to make any concessions	Stubborn and refuse to make any concessions	No deal. Despite the fact that there was a good solution available, you both walk away without a deal.
Defensive and hold your cards close to your chest	Defensive and hold their cards close to their chest	A sub-optimum deal. It is common 'wisdom' in negotiations not to give away any information. Actually, this ain't so wise. This approach leads to lower value solutions because the other party does not know how to help you get your best win. Plus, you miss the best deal available because you are both too suspicious.
Aggressive	Aggressive	A lose-lose deal. It rapidly becomes a fight and any deal agreed will simply not be implemented in the best way for either party.

It is only natural. But we can use this law to our advantage:

If you want them to:	You should:
Be open and honest	Be open and honest
Be trustworthy	Be trustworthy
Help you achieve your win	Help them achieve their win
Implement the deal in good faith	Implement the deal in good faith
Treat you with respect	Treat them with respect

Kind of makes sense, eh?

This is bad news and good news. The bad news is that it places responsibility for their behaviour on your shoulders. That is tough, it means you cannot blame them anymore for being unreasonable. If they are, perhaps it is in response to *you* being unreasonable in the first place.

But it is good news too because it now means you have a degree of control over their behaviour. If you want them to behave in a particular way, just behave that way yourself.

Is this a sure-fire, 100% guaranteed rule? No. There are no sure-fire, 100% guaranteed rules in life, I am afraid, your mum should have told you that already. But it will apply for the most part.

Trust engenders trust

Think about it. Your deals are important and, fair to say, you want to work with someone you can trust. Some deals are so important you want to work with someone you could trust with your life, someone you could trust with your *cojones*.

Now, think about this: do you really want to put your cojones in the hands of someone who does not actually trust *you*?

If they do not trust you, of course you cannot trust them. So the question is: are *you* trustworthy? Sorry to turn it back on you but they will never be reliable if they cannot trust you.

How much do *you* hide information? How much do you not tell the whole truth? How much do you rationalise your motives after just a teeny-weeny bit of deception (for their own good, of course, and it was only that one time and ... and...yeah, yeah, yeah!).

Trust engenders trust. If they can trust you, they are more likely to be trustworthy themselves, as simple as that. As Henry Ford nearly said, "If you think you can trust or you think you can't, you're probably right."

So, show you have integrity and show you will deliver. Listen to them before you start talking about what you want. Find out what is important to them and demonstrate that you will respect that. Ask questions around it to make sure your understanding is correct and full.

Under-promise, over-deliver. Be clear about what you can and cannot do, with explanations why. If you are clear in your 'no', they will trust your 'yes' much more. And then try to go that extra mile in your delivery. Keep your promises and be accountable for anything that goes wrong. If there is a mistake on your side put it right. If there is a mistake on their side, allow and forgive.

Sorry, it is tough, isn't it? But it will pay off. All of these will build their trust in you, and thereby increase their trustworthiness at the same time.

Be easily readable. This may run counter to the advice given by many old-school negotiating books but if you are poker-faced then they will not know what you are thinking... *and so they will not trust you.* Keep the poker-face for the poker table. Remember, if they cannot trust you, you sure as hell should not be placing any trust in them.

Share some information with them. If you really do not trust them, it may be worthwhile starting with something small or low-value. Take it step by step and build the trust at a comfortable pace.

Reciprocation is one of Cialdini's rules of influence, in fact it is the first. If you do someone a favour, they are likely to do you a favour in return. Interestingly, studies show that they are actually likely to do you a *bigger* favour in return. Share some information with them and they are likely to open up and share information with you. If you show generosity upfront, they are likely to be generous back.

Open-Book – Ricardo Semler, the Maverick

The traditional approach of secretively holding all your cards close to your chest can be counter-productive. The open-book approach, on the other hand, is a scary thought but can be incredibly powerful in building trust and, more importantly, in generating extra value and finding the best solution for everyone.

Perhaps its most successful proponent is Ricardo Semler who wrote about his story in the book 'Maverick'. Based in Sao Paulo, he took over his father's business, SEMCO, a manufacturing company, when he was 21 and grew it from annual revenues of $4m in 1981 to $35m in 1993 and $160m in 1999. And this against the backdrop of the Brazilian economic "lost decade".

His approach? Complete and total openness regarding all figures with everyone; with his customers, with his suppliers, with his employees and with the unions (Brazil is a particularly unionised country).

To give an example, his employees are allowed to decide their own wages. Yes, feel free to read that again, his employees decide their own wages. This sounds incredible and unworkable but, amazingly, it is successful.

It works partly because the same openness means that your decision about your salary is made within the context of full knowledge of the company's costs and revenue forecasts. Within that context, you can make a very accurate and fair estimate of what your job is worth economically. And it works partly because the same openness means the figure you set for yourself will be visible for everyone else to see.

In fact, the policy earned so much trust amongst the workforce that no one abused it, frequently resulting in real-term salary *reductions*.

> The honesty of the totally open-book approach leads to a great trust amongst all stakeholders and a tremendously motivated workforce. As a result, SEMCO's growth rate is exceptional.

Expect them to behave in good faith and they will

Mike Tyson is famous for being "the baddest man on the planet". Brought up in Brownsville, one of the worst ghettos of the Bronx, at the age of 12 he was arrested for the 38th time and sent to Spofford Juvenile Centre. In a highly controversial career, he would frighten opponents by telling them he wanted to eat their children (and he was pretty convincing too), and rather than aim for his opponent's face, he would aim for the *back* of the head. As well as being convicted and jailed for rape, he bit the ear of Evander Holyfield, has punched photographers, admitted to various drug addictions and been declared bankrupt.

And yet, on his release from prison, his very first act was to go to a mosque, kneel down at the feet of Muhammad Ali and serve him food. A pure and simple act of humility.

Bad Mike Tyson, Good Mike Tyson. Everybody has both sides to them. Which one will you meet? Much of it depends on you. If you say to Tyson, "Come on if you think you're hard enough", well you might get Bad Mike Tyson and you might regret it.

But relate to him as the person who did such an amazing thing on release from prison and you will find yourself dealing with Good Mike Tyson. How you relate to the other person drives how they behave to you.

And the only boxer more frightening than Tyson was George Foreman, 6ft 3½in of muscle, angry at the world and anyone who came near him. He is now an ordained minister and the smiley, cuddly guy who sells the Lean Mean Fat-Reducing Grilling Machine on television. Bad George Foreman, Good George Foreman.

Mostly, people do behave in good faith and this is true even with some of the tougher cookies if you behave in the right way with them.

So, be trustworthy and they will be trustworthy in kind. Moreover, *show* trust in the other person and they are likely to live up to it.

According to Cialdini, in one experiment a man is sitting on a busy beach, he goes for a swim, leaving his towel and belongings behind. Along comes a thief (part of the experiment) and takes his radio. 20% of the time, someone sitting nearby would get up and stop the thief. However, if the man first asked, "Excuse me, can you watch my things", 95% of people stopped the thief. By placing trust in the other person, they respond.

It is the secret to Warren Buffett's billions. He never sets targets for the chief executives of Berkshire Hathaway's companies. Instead, every year he asks them to set their own targets. He says they always set the bar much higher than he would have. And he leaves them to it and trusts them to deliver and rarely checks in again until the next year. They always deliver. He shows trust in them and they live up to it.

People live up to the expectation we have of them. It is a well-studied social phenomenon known as the Pygmalion Effect. Robert Rosenthal, a Harvard Professor, showed that if teachers were told that a particular group of students were high-achievers (even though they were picked randomly from an averagely performing class), that group of students would perform much better in their exams at the end of the year. In other words, the teachers expected them to do well and the students lived up to that expectation.

This really is another secret of the universe. We live up to our expectations. Expect someone to be trustworthy and they will live up to it.

 Action points

A high-trust co-operative approach is by the far the most effective method of getting the best deal you can. However, this is only true if the trust is well-placed. Your counterparty is likely to follow your lead in terms of attitude and behaviour.

▶ Build trust by sharing information and by being trustworthy yourself

▶ Share information, at a rate that you feel comfortable with, judging by their response in behaviour.

Pray together and bring a dog

There have been some interesting studies into which circumstances make people more honest.

In one experiment, Dan Ariely gave people a general knowledge test and had the answers marked and so was able to find the average number of correct scores, in this instance 4 out of 20. Next, he gave people the same test but afterwards gave out the answers and asked people to self-mark. Self-marking obviously made people more intelligent because, interestingly, the average increased to 7 out of 20.

He varied the circumstances of the test to see how they impacted people's honesty. Surprisingly, cheating did not increase with a monetary payment per correct answer. Nor was it linked to the likelihood of getting caught.

In one instance, though, a participant was actually an actor who stood up at the end of the test and said loudly that he got them all right. This did have a significant impact on the amount of cheating, depending on how the other participants saw him. If he was considered 'one of us' (because he was wearing the sweatshirt of their college), the amount of cheating would increase. But if he was considered an 'outsider' (because he was wearing the sweatshirt of a rival college), the amount of cheating would actually go down.

In another variation, he found there was no cheating at all if the questions were about the 10 Commandments! Nor did they cheat if the conversation prior to the test was about the 10 Commandments or if participants were told that, of course, the test was being conducted under the guidelines of the MIT Code of Honour. This, despite the fact there is no MIT Code of Honour.

Christoph Engel of the Max Planck Institute in Bonn also studied what makes a person generous. His studies verified the natural inclination that the more human-to-human the interaction, the more generosity. In other words, getting to know them better, building a stronger connection and, if needs be, taking the conversation away from the group and on to a one-to-one basis, will all increase their generosity. Showing you deserve such generosity also works in your favour. We shall return to Engel's work later for some more interesting findings.

Other studies showing ways to bring out people's better side revolve around The Prisoner's Dilemma. This is a mainstay of Game Theory where players can choose to collaborate (win-win) or to compete (win-lose) and has been researched extensively.

In one study, a group of people played the game after listening to a story of human atrocities; another group played the game after listening to a story of someone having their life saved with a kidney transplant donated by a complete stranger. The latter group collaborated much more than the former.

In another, Christopher Honts and Matthew Christensen at Central Michigan University used the Prisoner's Dilemma to study the effect of a dog's presence on people's behaviour. They found that people were 30% more likely to collaborate if a dog was around. They also found people were more likely to judge their fellow colleagues as co-operative and supportive if a dog was present. (Google, by the way, are one of a growing number of companies that allow or even encourage employees to bring their dogs to the office.).

It seems that certain things bring out the more honourable side of us. The MIT Code of Honour (whether it exists or not) and religious references seem to do so. So do dogs and uplifting stories.

Touch is yet another.

In a study reported by Barbara and Allen Pease, the University of Minnesota ran an experiment with two variations. The first involved a coin being left on the ledge of a public phone booth and, when an unsuspecting member of the public was in the booth, a researcher would appear and ask if they had seen a coin on the ledge. The second variation was identical except when the researcher asked about the coin, they also touched the person gently on the arm.

The first variation got a 23% success rate, the second, with the touch on the arm, got a 68% success rate. Touch increased the honesty of the other person *threefold*.

So lesson: bring a dog and hold hands while you say prayers at the beginning of the meeting.

Make the future more present

Ron Luciano was a famous Major League baseball umpire, described as "one of the few umpires people have paid their way into the park to see." In his biography, he tells how, if he ever had a hangover, he would ask the catcher to do the umpiring for him. If it was a strike, the catcher would hold the ball a little longer; if it was a ball, the catcher would throw it straight back. Luciano could be so sure that the catcher would play ball (as it were) because he knew there was plenty of opportunity to get revenge should they ever try to get away with anything!

The likelihood of co-operation can be enhanced by making the future more present. You can do this by:

• emphasising future dealings (whether of a directly similar nature or not)
• make any lock-in period longer
• making future possible transactions larger or of greater value
• making interactions sooner and more frequent
• by limiting the numbers of other people that either you or they deal with.

All of these methods will give greater importance to future interactions and therefore incentivise them to play fair in this interaction at hand.

Breaking the transaction down into smaller parts can help, too, so if they do cheat, it is only on a small step and you can invoke your retaliation sooner. Instead of letting them pay everything after all of the goods have been delivered, deliver smaller amounts and have them pay after receipt of each delivery. This way, they are still incentivised to pay because they need the rest of the deliveries. Also, the amount that is at risk is much smaller. What is more, with each successful delivery and payment, you are building up a track record of trust and trustworthiness on both sides. If you can, structure it so you have to do as little of your side of the deal until they have done their side of the deal.

Action points

People are more likely to be co-operative and trustworthy if they know they will be doing business with you again in the future. Consequently,

▶ Emphasise the likelihood that you will be dealing with them again

▶ If you feel you need to, structure the deal so that the minimum is at risk if they do renege.

7.2 CHANNEL THEIR SELF-INTEREST

Probably the most powerful way of getting co-operative behaviour is to channel the self-interest of your negotiating partner. Find the link between their win and yours and, as they work towards theirs, they will help bring about yours. Easy. Except people are surprisingly dim at identifying their own win and you often have to do the thinking for them.

Even then, use short words as you explain it. It is one of the slightly disappointing aspects of our world that ideas do not succeed on the basis of their quality but on the basis of how well they are put across. You may have a wonderful solution that gives your counterparty all they ever wanted and yet, far too frequently, they will still say no, for whatever reason that makes some strange kind of sense in their funny little brain.

We have already seen many of the sub-skills of influence. Rapport is the sine qua non. Credibility, likewise. And much of the preparation is about building your case to persuade.

But, here in the meeting, perhaps the best and simplest way is to ask your counterparty directly what they are trying to achieve and then make sure you frame your message in those terms.

Give them what they want and you have a deal

In 1980, Fidel Castro relaxed the restrictions on leaving Cuba and so began what became known as the "Mariel Boatlift" in which nearly 125,000 Cubans left for America. Craftily, Castro released many prisoners from jails and mental institutions, allowing them to leave for the States. American courts judged about 2,500 refugees to be unfit for asylum so held them for deporting back to their home country.

Of course, this was the last thing the asylum-seekers wanted and they caused riots in various holding institutions across the country. In Talladega Federal Correction Institution in Alabama, there were very dangerous men involved, having track records of murder and other violent crimes. They seized a number of employees and barricaded themselves in,

---

demanding guarantees they would not be sent home.

Gary Noesner, a senior FBI officer, was brought in to negotiate with them. For days the talks went nowhere. Neither side gave an inch.

As time passed, however, the rioters naturally became hungrier. Noesner decided to open up a new front in the stand-off. One morning, he ordered the prison staff to fry bacon and brew coffee. The smells floated through the prison. Rioter stomachs gurgled loudly. The next lunchtime, a large grill was set up to cook hamburgers for the riot police. Rioter stomachs gurgled seismically.

A cruel ploy but effective. Later that night, an inmate called on the phone: "We want to talk. Outside. Right now."

If they are hungry and you have food, you have a deal.

Building a frame to persuade

What do you do if they are not hungry?

The first point to make is do not give up too easily – a successful salesperson will tell you that "No" does not mean "Never", it means "Not yet". That is, they have not been persuaded yet. Resistance to an idea is often an expression of *ambivalence* rather than outright opposition, in which case work on strengthening the merits of your case.

Lyle Sussman says you build a frame to persuade. And you do this in four steps:

1. Identify your objective
2. Conduct SWOT analysis *on the other party*
3. Determine the other party's core values
4. Write a simple, vivid statement that links the above.

The beauty of this approach is that it uses the dynamics of *their* situation to reach *your* objectives. You use their strengths, weaknesses, opportunities, threats and values to make your objectives the convincing route forward.

And use vivid, colourful language. In one experiment, jurors were asked to arbitrate on a contractual disagreement where, unbeknown to the jurors, both contractor and sub-contractor were acting from a script. There were two versions of the script which were identical in content but one used more colourful language than the other (for example, using the word 'jagged' instead of 'rough'). The jurors found in favour of the contractor *twice as frequently* when they used colourful language.

Emotional words can be effective too. Emotions have a place in negotiations. In Camp David in 1978, the talks between Menachim Begin, the Prime Minister of Israel, and Anwar Sadat, the Egyptian President, were still facing difficulties even on the last day. In Jimmy Carter's book, Talking Peace, he describes:

"In the end, something unexpected almost miraculously helped to break the deadlock. We had made some photos of the three of us and Begin has asked me to sign one for each of his eight grandchildren. Sadat had already signed them. My secretary suggested that I personalise them and on each of them I wrote the name of one grandchild above my signature. Although Begin had become quite unfriendly towards me because of the pressure I was putting on him and Sadat, I decided to take the photographs over to his cabin personally. As he looked at the pictures and read the names aloud, he became very emotional. He was thinking, I am sure, about his responsibility to his people and about what happens to children in war. Both of us had tears in our eyes."

Shortly afterwards, Begin agreed to all of the remaining contested points and the accords were signed that day.

Seeding your ideas before the negotiation

Like a ship at sea, it takes people a while to change direction so if you are trying to persuade them, do not expect them to change their mind instantly. **Give them a chance to think about your idea and come around in their own time.**

If you need an answer in the upcoming meeting, find ways to get your message across beforehand. Sell your idea outside of the negotiation room then it will not be new to them when you meet. If you are lucky they will even present it back to you as *their* idea. Why is that lucky? Because then they will truly own it and you will be sure they will implement it. As Harry Truman said, "It's amazing what you can accomplish if you do not care who gets the credit."

Send them pre-meeting material, suggest it on the phone, chat about it at the coffee machine. Get out the map of their world that you drew as part of your preparation (you did, didn't you?) and look to see what indirect ways you can get your message to them. Who do they talk to that you can talk to? Who do they listen to that you can reach?

You can do this under the guise of soliciting information, it is much easier to get someone's time and listening if you are asking questions rather than overtly pushing an idea. The very act of questioning, though, can itself be a vehicle for the selling.

Using questions to persuade

Questions, in general, are an unintrusive but powerful way to persuade. Remember the other party has come to the negotiation table for a reason. Questions that keep these reasons to the front of their mind will maintain their motivation towards a deal.

Now, people fall into two camps; they are either motivated *away from* problems and risks or *towards* goals and benefits. So, to catch both personality types, ask questions about both.

Ask questions about the problem they are facing that brings them to the negotiation table. Explore it, each question you ask about the problem keeps it in the foreground of their mind and reminds them why they are here.

But you can go further. Ask questions about the impact, it will *increase* their drive to do a deal. Exploring the possible knock-on effects of the problem magnifies any motivation they have for resolving it.

- Car mechanic: I noticed the brakes were squeaky, we could fix that while you're here. It won't cost a lot.
- Customer: I know, I need to sort them out. But I'm a bit short of cash at the moment so I will do it later.
- Car mechanic: Ok. What do you think the problem is?
- Customer: Well, I'm sure you know. They're old and worn and need replacing soon.
- Car mechanic: What could happen if you don't replace them?
- Customer: Well, I suppose, the worst-case scenario is they could fail on me and I could get involved in some sort of a crash.
- Car mechanic: Is it just yourself in the car normally?

-     Customer: No, actually. My wife usually drives it, she takes the kids to school in it. Hmm, maybe I should sort them out now. Go on, it won't take long, will it?

By exploring the problem and then the potential implications, the car mechanic was able to persuade the customer to go from "I will get round to it soon" to "I will do it now".

This works with people motivated away from problems and risks. You can also increase their "towards" motivation by asking about the benefits of striking the deal and then the possible implications of these.

-     Customer: I think that's too expensive, I can decorate the house myself.
-     Decorator: Sure, it probably makes a lot of sense. What made you ring us in the first place?
-     Customer: Well, obviously you would do a more professional job than me and perhaps you could do some things that I wouldn't be able to do at all.
-     Decorator: And why is that important to you?
-     Customer: Well, I'm decorating it because I want to sell it and, of course, the nicer it looks the faster it will go.
-     Decorator: Is there any other reason why you wanted a professional in to do the job?
-     Customer: Yes, you said you could start straight away and you would get it finished within the week. That would be great, I could have people viewing the place next weekend.
-     Decorator: Why do you want to sell it quickly?
-     Customer: Well, I'm moving abroad and the sooner I sell up, the sooner I can go. I'm really excited about it, I want to go now! How much did you say again? Maybe we can strike a deal after all...

These questions took the customer's mind to the benefits of striking a deal. Again, the questioning took it further and the deeper into the benefits it went, the greater the energy for the deal. We can see in this example a hierarchy of benefits:

> Level 1 benefit: do professional job
> Level 1 benefit: finish the job quicker
> Level 2 benefit: sell the house quicker
> Level 3 benefit: move abroad quicker and start new life straight away.

The first level benefits helped motivate them, the second level benefits motivated them even more. But it was not until the discussion moved to the third level of benefits that the customer became really excited and decided to strike the deal.

The other party's incentive to come to a win-win agreement comes from the gap between the problem they are currently facing and solution that the deal would bring them. The larger they perceive this gap, the greater the incentive. These questions not only keep the problem and the solution in the forefront of their mind, they also magnify the potential problem and magnify the potential solution and thereby increase their incentive to a deal.

Furthermore, the beauty of this approach is that you have not overtly tried to persuade them at all. You have only asked questions and, in answering them, they have convinced themselves. This is a much more effective way of convincing.

Don't shoot the dog

Karen Pryor has written a marvellous book on changing behaviour called "Don't Shoot the Dog" and her methods can be very powerful in bringing the other party around to a win-win approach.

Pryor was a student of B.F. Skinner, of behavioural conditioning fame. Skinner's idea was that behaviour could be developed by punishing the behaviour you did not want to see and rewarding the behaviour you did. And with this method, he trained rats to run through mazes and pigeons to play table-tennis. Apparently, his students tested the model on himself – every time he lectured from the left-hand side of the stage, they would smile, nod and look attentive; every time he lectured from the right-hand side, they would frown, look down and uninterestedly rummage in their bags. The story goes that he nearly fell off the left-hand side of the stage.

Pryor got a job as a dolphin trainer and brought similar methods to the job. Her variation was to ignore negative behaviour rather than punish it because she found punishment counter-productive.

A new dolphin would enter the pool, swim around and, when it did something interesting like jump out of the water, she would throw it a fish. The dolphin would be pleased but would not make the connection.

A little later, it might jump out of the water again and again she would throw it a fish. The same a third time and perhaps by now the dolphin would make the connection and start continuously jumping out of the water.

Once that trick had been learnt, Pryor would stop rewarding it. The dolphin would be confused – "Hold on, why aren't I getting any fish?". But maybe it would do something else interesting, swim on its back, for example, and Pryor would reward that. "Hmm," thought the dolphin. It would swim on its back again and get another fish. "Now, I'm getting fish for swimming on my back. What's going on?". Of course, once it had learnt that trick, too, Pryor would stop rewarding it. The dolphin would be confused again.

According to Pryor, after it had learnt a few tricks in this manner, the dolphin would eventually click (well, that *is* what dolphins do). She says they would go mad, swimming around excitedly doing all kinds of tricks just to show off what they could do – juggling whilst riding a unicycle and reciting the works of Shakespeare (in dolphin, obviously).

She went on to train many other animals and describes similar results with each and she has contributed significantly to the spread of "clicker" training for dogs, probably the most common form of dog-training, which uses similar principles.

Now, evidently, you are unlikely to be negotiating with a dolphin. But it turns out that what works for dolphins, rats, pigeons and dogs, also works for negotiators. Of course, you need a different reward system. Throwing a fish at them or clicking a clicker is unlikely to impress your co-negotiator (feel free to experiment, though).

In a negotiation the reward, of course, could be a concession but it does not need to be. It is usually something as simple as thanks or acknowledgement; simpler still, a supportive nod of the head. But such positive marking of the behaviour reinforces it and makes it more likely to happen again.

Labelling the behaviour as an identity trait also works. Let us say they suggest a solution to one of the areas of dispute; if you say that they are a good problem-solver, you are likely to get more of that behaviour.

Try this every time your counterparty does something that has a win-win flavour and do not be surprised if very soon he is juggling whilst riding a unicycle and reciting the works of Shakespeare (in dolphin).

Understanding group dynamics to influence

What do you do if, as is frequently the case, there is more than one person in the room? The answer, according to the work of Michael Grinder, is to identify three types of people and work with them. They are the leader, the advisor and the barometer.

The leader of the group is the most important, they are the final decision-maker, and it is they whom you need to persuade primarily. They are usually obvious by their behaviour – they are likely to be the first to sit down and the first to pick up their papers to leave, they are likely to both open and close the conversation and they are likely to be the person that talks the most.

But not always so. More tellingly, the leader is revealed by other people's reaction to them. Others will show noticeable deference to the leader, they will agree with them, they will stop talking if the leader talks over them and they will usually look at the them and listen observably as they speak.

Target the leader but not always directly. The second important type of person is the advisor. This is the person who the leader listens to and seeks advice from on certain matters. They can be an oblique route to your target. Engage with them and persuade them and they will do the work on the leader.

And the third type of person is the barometer. The barometer is the person who is the quickest to show the group's thinking and they can be a useful way to read the leader's mind. The barometer thinks the same way as the leader but are easier to read, either because they are quicker of thought or because they are more expressive in their reaction. As a result, you can tune into their responses (verbal or non-verbal) to gauge how well your arguments are working.

Let us say you are talking about something contentious and you notice the barometer starts moving around on his chair in an agitated manner. The leader has not expressed anything but you still know that he has a concern from *the barometer's* behaviour. Armed with this, you can pro-actively acknowledge the concern ("I'm sure some of you are thinking…") and address it. They will be impressed.

And not only may there be more than one person in the room, there may be more than one *group* in the room. You may have operations staff present, for example, and the finance team. In larger negotiations there can be many teams involved and each will have different criteria and different motivations and you will need to address all of them.

The process is the same: for each group, identify the three types of people. Read the barometer, persuade the advisor but your target is the leader.

Even deadly enemies can be turned around

To quote George Mitchell, "At the heart of all the problems in Northern Ireland is mistrust. Centuries of conflict have generated hatreds that make it virtually impossible to trust each other".

After centuries of mistrust, is it any wonder it took years to re-build it. The talks that led up to the Good Friday Agreement took three years. And that was after years of other talks paving way for these.

Simon Horton

The final deadline was set for Good Friday 1998 and it was not until the end of this day that Mitchell knew he had success. For the whole three years up until this point, though his remit was to be publicly optimistic, he had no idea whether they would succeed or not such was the bad feeling between all parties.

But finally peace was agreed.

And in an almost miraculous turn around trust was re-built. Ian Paisley became First Minister of Northern Ireland and Martin McGuinness, his deadly enemy, became his Deputy.

They ended up working remarkably well together, to the extent that they were known as The Chuckle Brothers, such was the lightness and humour with which they worked together. After Paisley retired, McGuinness admitted to telephoning him for advice and even just to see how he was.

It can take time to build trust. But the return on the investment makes it worth it.

 Action points

You can move them to win-win by helping them find their win and making the link between yours and theirs. You may need to do the thinking for them and you may need to use your best influencing skills:

▸ Step into their shoes and frame your message accordingly
▸ Frame it in terms of their SWOT
▸ Ask questions rather than tell
▸ Observe any group dynamics and use them to your favour.

7.3 DEALING WITH DIFFICULT PEOPLE

If you take the approach that has been described in the book so far, the other party *is* likely to adopt a win-win strategy too. Even if they originally had quite a different mind-set, the techniques in this book really will turn people around.

But some people can be quite stubbornly *not* win-win and there will be instances where they just do not play the game. They can be unreasonable, they can be unwilling to compromise, unwilling to accept a 'fair' deal, they can be personally abusive, even aggressive, they can be manipulative or hold back information, they can lie, they can use tricks, they may use their muscle simply because they can.

So in this section, we will look at how to deal with these.

Manage your response

The first thing to do is manage your own emotional response so you can choose your optimum strategy in a reasoned way.

Jonathan Cohen, a neuro-economist at Princeton, has studied what actually occurs in the brain during economic transactions. During the Ultimatum Game, for example, if someone is offered less than they consider a fair amount, the emotional part of the brain, the amygdala, kicks in and we get angry. Shortly afterwards, the pre-frontal cortex may step in and over-ride the anger with a more detached, logical reaction.

Cohen says some people are better at regulating the emotional response than others. In a negotiation, you want to be in control of your emotions so you make the right decisions. If you are dealing with someone who is not playing the game, let your pre-frontal cortex run the show.

Mostly, people respond out of habit. As such, we tend either to fight back, give in or walk away from the negotiation – the evolutionary fight/flight/freeze response of the amygdala. We are not in control of this, it is our pattern rather than a thought-through response.

Whichever your fight/flight/freeze response, it is not the Strong Win-Win way. Why not? Because you are not in control of automatic responses, they are just programmes that run you. Strong win-win says evaluate which of these is appropriate at any given time. then put it into practice in a managed way. This is not easy and some of you will find it difficult to be more assertive when you need to be and some of you will find it difficult to be generous when you need to be and some of you will find it difficult to walk away when you need to.

But by thinking consciously about how we react, we retain control of the programme. To do this, first pause. Do not react immediately but instead take a breather. Timothy Gallwey, author of the celebrated "Inner Game" series of books, says "STOP!".

S – Step back

T – Think

O – Organise your thoughts

P – Proceed when you know your best action.

Remember, you do not have to answer immediately. You can:

- o   pause simply in the moment
- o   hand over to a negotiating partner in your team
- o   call for a time-out
- o   break off until the next meeting.

As you evaluate your possible actions, remember to stay focussed on your outcome from the deal. Even the pause itself can be enough to change the dynamic. If they are shouting at you or being abusive and you refuse to reply in kind but simply wait until they finish and then sit there quietly for a further 10 to 15 seconds, it can be enough to show up their behaviour without actively labelling it. It will often bring them around to a more reasonable approach.

As Fisher and Ury say in "Getting to Yes", separate the person from the behaviour. Make all constructive (ok, negative) judgements about the behaviour or results and not about the person. On the other hand, make all positive judgements about *them*. Compare "shouting is not helpful" and "this clause here needs changing" with "you can be very diplomatic" and "that's a good idea of yours". The first two are constructive and strictly about the behaviour or thing and the second two are positive and relate to the individual person.

Of course, if they are being especially difficult, this can be challenging. I had one friend who worked as a mediator between trades unions and management and he said that both parties would be incredibly abusive to him as though it was all his fault, personally. They would say tremendously rude things straight to his face but it would never affect him. He would imagine they were primitives throwing sticks and stones at him and would mentally duck out of the way and think "Oh, that's interesting they said that" but not let it affect him.

If it is a personal attack, do not respond defensively. Pause, the silence may embarrass them. If necessary, break the mood by suggesting a break. Or ignore the comment and stay with the issue at hand, re-directing the attack on you to an attack on the problem. Use "we" language rather than "you" and "me".

Remind them of why they are here

If you want a successful deal and they are not playing win-win, it is up to you to show them the benefits (to them) of doing so. Remind them of why they are there at the negotiating table. Remind of their bigger picture interests. Remind them of why what you are offering is of benefit to them. Remind them of their alternatives, what they would be left with if you walked away. You may even have to dollarise it, put figures to it, to spell it out clearly.

William Ury, co-author of 'Getting to Yes', also wrote 'Getting Past No', which is specifically about turning people around when they are not playing the game. He says if you want people to be more reasonable and win-win orientated, you may have to do the thinking for them. If what you are offering really is a good deal, this should be enough to bring them to their senses but you may just have to spell it out.

Be strong in the deal...

Now, more than ever, credibility is critical – you need to be strong in the deal and earn their respect. The Strong Win-Win view is never let yourself be bullied.

Bear in mind, bullies bully people who ask to be bullied. Perhaps that is harsh but we can certainly say bullies bully people when they think they can get away with it. It is important they know you will not tolerate it.

This is a key part of the Strong Win-Win philosophy. Act credible and they are much more likely to treat you with respect. Being strong in the deal is essential.

So remember all the material about displaying credibility; the stronger you come across, the more they will treat you with respect.

. ...And focus on the relationship

And, of course, there is still the balance to be found between being strong in the deal and focussing on the relationship. If you are strong *and* you have a good relationship you will get your best deal.

If the difficult behaviour is through email or letter, respond by telephone or, better still, face to face. Get human to human. Mention a common friend, remind them of your common Scottish ancestry or your shared love of sericulture. Remind them you are 'one of us' and they will probably change their tune.

Try to understand their behaviour

Try to see it from their point of view – who knows, they may have a good point. Even if not, if you acknowledge how they see it, that will take a lot of the wind out of their sails.

Actively listen and ask questions to recognise where they are coming from. Play back to them your understanding and ask have you missed anything. Show you appreciate their feelings and tell them that, if you were in their shoes, you would probably feel the same.

Look for what you can agree with but do all of this confidently and standing up for your own views at the same time. It does not mean that you have to give in to their pressure, it just means acknowledge how they see things. We often dismiss our opponent's demands as irrational or unfair but this is not true. They have a rationality, it just might not be yours. Find out their drivers, find out their reasoning and work with it.

Breakthrough in the Northern Ireland peace process

Acknowledgement of the other party's views and feelings can really change the whole dynamic. In 1993, a joint statement was issued by the British and Irish governments, recognising the other parties' concerns re the Northern Ireland situation and their commitment to addressing them. This changed the tone from conflict to acknowledgement. As

---

> a result, the IRA could no longer see the UK government as a military enemy and were able to renounce all military activity. A major breakthrough. The Unionists responded. Peace could finally be countenanced.

Appreciate their concerns

Roger Fisher is also the author of "Beyond Reason", in which he looks at the role of emotions in negotiation, and he believes that a core emotional concern of many negotiators is that they are appreciated. Taking the time and making the effort to appreciate the other person can have a massive effect on the communication.

To appreciate:

1)   Really listen to their point of view
2)   Listen to the sub-text of their communication
3)   Listen for the emotion
4)   See the merit in their position
5)   Communicate that you understand and see the merit

Important: you can appreciate their point of view and still appreciate your own. Appreciation does not mean giving in. However, it does open up the communication to a completely different level.

People's behaviour is never in isolation, it is in response to the behaviour of someone else. If you want to change someone else's behaviour, often the easiest way is to change yours. So consider just how you may have contributed to their behaviour and how you can change that.

Milton Erickson, the great American clinical therapist, described how when growing up on his father's farm, his father tried to get a calf into the barn. The calf was extremely stubborn and no matter how hard Erickson's father pulled, he could not pull him inside. Erickson, just a boy, thought of a different idea. He tried pulling the calf *out* of the barn. Of course, that stubborn calf just pulled back even harder, and slowly it pulled itself and Erickson into the barn.

If they have been stubbornly defending a position that is untenable, pushing harder is not necessarily going to make any difference. Try changing tack in some way and they, necessarily, will change tack too and you may just get your result.

Take the neutral perspective

We have just seen how powerful it can be to see things from their perspective. It can also be very useful to take a neutral perspective. Mentally step outside of the situation, into the fly-on-the-wall position, and look at the two parties as if they were 'over there'. From this perspective, what can you see?

Imagine being a mediator: if you had to mediate between these two parties, what would you suggest to each? Whilst you have your point of view and your interests to be met, if you stay stuck in that position (and they stay stuck in theirs), it could be you do not progress. If you imagine how a mediator would handle it, it may enable you to move forward.

Allow them a way out

A lot of negotiation is about face. You need to treat everyone with respect and everyone as a high status individual. Making a concession can impact a person's self-image because it makes them feel weak so they are naturally loathe to do this. Giving them respect will make them feel better about themselves and so they will not be worried about making concessions.

Give them respect so you can get a better deal. And, of course, give yourself respect too. They will only appreciate the respect you give them if it comes from someone who respects themselves.

Help them make a concession by showing that circumstances have changed and the new circumstances support the changed position (even if it is the Tuesday reason – "Well, of course, its now taking place on Tuesday and Tuesdays are more expensive".)

Give them a way out that enables them to back down with grace. Make it their idea – giving them credit for it is often all you need for them to take it on. So explore their ideas and build on them. Say your idea sprung from something they said. Give them a choice of options – when they choose, it is now their idea.

You may also need to help them sell it in. Maybe that is the explanation for their unreasonable behaviour, that their internal constituency are being unreasonable. Work with them on strategies, arguments and independent benchmarks that will bring these third parties on board.

Talk to the people you need to

In 1998, the closer the Northern Ireland peace talks got to agreement, the more bombs were going off that looked to threaten the whole process. Vested interests were probably to play, many people did not necessarily want to see a return to law and order. It was causing a lot of tension and mistrust amongst the parties trying to come to an agreement. Mo Mowlam, the British Secretary of State for Northern Ireland, went to the Maze Prison to visit the prisoners. These had a special position amongst the people of Northern Ireland. They were generally considered heroes, they were the hardest of the hard, they were the most likely to be against the process. But by meeting them face to face she pulled off a coup and they came out in public support of the peace process.

Call them on their behaviour

Whilst no excuse, sometimes people act aggressively or abusively without realising. Other times it is because they think they can get away with it and sometimes it is because they are desperate.

Calling them on their behaviour, with varying degrees of diplomacy, can shine a light on what they are doing and force them to reconsider their approach.

Even in extreme, you do not have to lose your temper but a firm statement of your position will be more effective: "Listen, I am happy to continue negotiating but not like this. Either we can negotiate on a more reasonable basis or we can reconvene until a later date when you are ready to negotiate in good faith."

Tit-For-Tat

Fisher and Ury believe that the principle-centred approach, as outlined in 'Getting to Yes' and 'Getting Past No' is usually enough to help people behave reasonably.

The Strong Win-Win philosophy agrees but believes combining it with Tit-For-Tat toughens it up.

Supported by some game-changing research by Robert Axelrod, which we will see later, the Tit-For-Tat strategy says be open and trusting and co-operative at first but if the other party lets you down, punish them in your next dealings with them. Now dealings does not mean deal. It can be the next meeting you have. But the principle is to start by co-operating and assuming co-operation on their part; continue co-operating as long as they co-operate; but as soon as they act negatively, retaliate.

Dr Mike Webster has helped design the FBI programmes on hostage negotiation. He promotes this parallel approach to crisis resolution, combining the promise of reward for good behaviour and the threat of penalty for bad behaviour, as the best method to bring the other party around.

It is carrot-and-stick, we all know it. You also need to be clear about this so that they know the impact of their behaviour and your threats and your promises need to be credible, which means following through on them.

But this way, you incentivise them to act in good faith. If they want the best deal on the table, they need to act in good faith to get it.

Axelrod suggested the following rules as a basis for a winning strategy:

1. Be nice: start by co-operating and continue co-operating as long as they do
2. Be provocable: retaliate as soon as they defect
3. Forgive: co-operate again when they resume co-operation
4. Be clear: let them know what you are doing and why so they know what to expect.
5. Do not be envious: don't worry about how much they get, maximise how much you get.

Subsequent research has suggested that real world situations produce better results if they follow the strategy of Tit-For-Tat+1. The plus one, in this instance, means not retaliating immediately if provoked but allowing the other party a chance to make amends.

This is because real world situations are often complex and allow "noise" into the system. So the action as intended and the action as interpreted are not always one and the same. Consequently, it is best not to go nuclear straightaway. Instead, communicate what has happened, communicate that it is not acceptable but give them a chance to explain or apologise or undo. If they repeat the behaviour, then you retaliate.

Using the plus one as a buffer in this manner prevents situations becoming hostile unnecessarily, through accident or misinterpretation.

Sukhwinder Shergill, at University College London, conducted a highly illuminating experiment in 2003 which illustrates how conflicts can escalate rapidly, even though neither side wishes it and both sides think they are behaving perfectly fairly.

His experiment involved two volunteers taking turns to apply pressure to the other's finger. The instruction was to give exactly the same pressure to the other person, as you felt you received. No more, no less. In practice, however, each person gave on average 40% more pressure than they had just received. This happened every turn so the situation escalated rapidly in spite of both sides genuinely thinking they were being fair and the other party was out of order.

How often do real-world scenarios with your partner, your boss, your negotiating counterparty mirror this behaviour precisely? What seems legitimate from one perspective appears belligerent to the other.

Tit-for-tat+1 gives an escape route and reduces the chances of needless escalation.

Last resorts

If you are still not making any progress, take stock and re-consider whether you want to continue. Why are you negotiating in the first place? What is your bigger picture goal? What is your Plan B and what is your counterparty currently offering? Which is, in reality, the better?

In this light, do you still want to negotiate?

If you do, what power can you bring to play that may force them to be more reasonable? See the chapter on power for an in-depth exploration of different sources of power available to you.

However, power should be used as a last resort and needs to be done skilfully because using it is often counter-productive. If you use power, they are very likely to use power in response and it will rapidly go downhill. According to Roger Fisher, you need to make it easy for them to say yes at the same time as you make it hard for them to say no. That is, always leave your best offer visible for them.

Do not assume they have thought through the implications of not agreeing. It is best to do it in a neutral, non-threatening kind of way. Ask them "What do you think will happen if...?", "What will you do if...?", "What do you think I will do if...?", "If you were in my shoes, what would you do if...?", "What do you think my boss will demand that I do if...?". These are not threats. Threats, to repeat, will be counter-productive and people do not respond to them. Instead, objectively make apparent and explore.

And, in the last resort, if you have to, act accordingly.

 **Action points**

If the other party is being difficult:

▸ Stay calm and manage your response

▸ Stay positive towards the relationship but under no circumstances let them bully you into an unnecessary concession

▸ Remind them of the benefits of the deal compared to the alternatives

▸ Act as a mediator would

▸ But if you are still getting no joy, consider your Plan B and at what point it is best to walk away.

CHAPTER 8:SOLVE THE PROBLEM

8.1 PROBLEM-SOLVING

So we have built rapport and established our credibility and we have shared what we all want from the deal. Now we have to come up with a solution that everyone is prepared to sign up for.

This is the tricky bit, isn't it? This is the real negotiation. This is the haggle, the arm-wrestle. This is the part where you have to watch for their dirty tricks and maybe have to pull a few yourself.

Well, maybe not. Maybe, if you have done everything else we have talked about to date and you have done it properly, maybe this is the *easy* bit. Maybe everything just falls into place. Maybe you do not even notice going through this stage. I have a colleague who conducted negotiations in the hundreds of millions of pounds and would come out with a deal but wondering quite how he got there. There seemed to be a nice chat then somehow an agreement was struck.

If all parties are working together for a win-win result and there is a reasonable degree of trust, then it does not have to be difficult. It does not have to involve smoke-filled rooms, late night stare-outs, banging the table, storming out and slamming doors.

Imagine it more like those 19th century diplomats who charmingly and politely carved up whole continents between them over tea and scones. "You take Danzig, old boy, we'll have Upper Silesia, then we'll sort out the Austro-Hungarian Empire after a jolly game of croquet".

Remember the Arm Game? Each person gets one point if the other person's hand touches the table – almost everyone defaults to an arm-wrestle and they get three or four points and a sore elbow. Better, say to the other guy "Let's work together on this one, mate" and everyone gets ten times as many points.

In this way, we reframe the negotiation as a problem to be solved together with the other parties. Great, everybody loves cracking a problem; think of it as a crossword puzzle or a Sudoku.

The negotiation process

Let us step back for a moment and see how this problem-solving fits into the whole process of the negotiation and there are different ways we can view it.

Zartman and Berman (1982) suggest there are three phases to a deal:

-       the pre-negotiation
-       the formula
-       the details.

The pre-negotiation involves those communications and correspondence that bring the negotiation into being. These "talks about talks" can be as short as 5 minutes or they can take years, in the case of long-standing international disputes.

They will include clarification of the scope of the discussions, who needs to be involved, and practical considerations such as venue and dates. They may also include whether any third parties will need to be present, such as mediators, arbitrators, observers or regulators.

In the formula section, you will agree the principles that the rest of the negotiations will adhere to. You will agree the process of the talks, the rules and statutes to be followed and any objective benchmarks, formulae and precedents that will provide the reference points of the bargaining process. The bargaining itself has not yet started.

Needless to say, these different phases are not set in stone, negotiations are never linear. Part of their value, however, is that it is usually easier to agree the principles up-front before anything substantive is being discussed and a win-win process and formula can usually be arrived at. Then, once they have been agreed, the negotiations themselves will ensue more smoothly by following the agreed process and reaching a fair outcome accordingly.

Looking at the process from a different angle, it can be useful to identify four phases:

•   Opening
•   Exploring
•   Problem-solving
•   Closing.

Again, they are rarely so cleanly defined and they usually overlap. Negotiations, to repeat, are not linear.

In the opening, the emphasis should be on nothing more than establishing rapport and credibility and the personal connection we discussed at length in chapter 6. The closing section we will address in chapter 9.

In the exploring section, we establish the nature of the problem that is to be solved. So start the substantive discussions by finding out what their win might be. And be sure to find this at the level of interests, not at the level of position. Start by finding out the background, what is going on for them, what are the problems they are currently facing, what are they trying to achieve over the next year or two years. If you know their bigger picture goals, you can help them achieve them. And if you show that you can help them with their goals, they will return the favour. Place all parties' goals and constraints on the table and you have defined your problem.

If you find your counterparty is old-school and they respond by putting their opening position on the table, that is fine. Ignore it. Instead, enquire the reasons behind it and ask what are they trying to achieve and what for? They may not even have consciously thought of this. This will take them to their bigger picture goal and will open a bigger discussion with more options for win-win, where they get a *better* deal than through their original positional approach.

They may be quite wary of giving this kind of information early on in the talks. Again, fine, it simply means you have not yet built sufficient trust. Stress that by knowing their interests you can help them achieve them better and build the trust by sharing your interests first..

You will want to share your interests anyway. Then, having established the interests of all parties, ask what ways could you help them achieve theirs and what ways could they help you achieve yours?

Now, already, you have the beginnings of a strategy for reaching win-win.

Work together as a partnership

So let us say we have established rapport and credibility and we have defined the problem to be solved: enable both players to maximise their points in the Arm Game; complete a trade so both sides are better off; resolve a border dispute peacefully and fairly.

Now work together to find the best solution. Work together as a partnership against the mutual challenge. You have an agenda and constraints, they have an agenda and constraints; you have ideas; they have ideas; you have resources, they have resources; you have contacts, they have contacts. Share them and solve the problem.

Hey, it can be enjoyable.

Of course, "a partnership isn't always 'hold hands and walk off into the sunset'" – a quote from a survey conducted by UMIST, the UK Institute of Logistics and A.T. Kearney, researching the nature of purchaser/supplier partnerships. From the same study, another quote, more blunt: "there's a lot of screwing going on in partnerships".

But it also found that the more effective partnerships included:

- sharing demand forecasts with suppliers
- actively helping its suppliers reduce costs
- actively helping its suppliers improve quality
- communicating directly with the suppliers' suppliers
- sharing data on its own inventory levels
- working with suppliers to reduce inventory in chain
- working together on product design

These suggest quite a close degree of integration between the parties. And if you can achieve this degree of working side-by-side, your negotiations will be very productive.

Interestingly, the study noted that often effective partnerships were formed at the operational level but would be sabotaged when the sales and purchasing departments got involved. That is, the professional negotiators would *undermine* strong effective partnerships already formed and working.

It is a shame: the human beings could work together, the negotiators could not. Remember: you are a human being too. (Probably. You never know who gets hold of a book these days.)

Working as a partnership does not mean going soft. Their win does not have to be at your expense; we are not talking lose-win. It seems strange to have to emphasise this but I will: MAKE SURE YOU GET YOUR WIN.

But nor does it mean win-lose. Your win does not have to be at their expense. Indeed, you will get a better win if you work together as a partnership, trying to crack a problem.

Be human but do not be soft. Be tough. Be tough on the problem together, be tough on getting the best win-win solution. This is why some companies enjoy working with the likes of Walmart. Their hard-hitting approach forces them to innovate and invent new solutions.

A colleague of mine was a negotiator for one of the world's largest construction companies. He found himself in a meeting where an important client, an airport company that owned several of the world's largest airports, demanded a re-negotiation of their contract: the same service at 20% reduction in cost.

My colleague said afterwards this was not an aggressive gesture, that the client offered to help find these reductions. And he admitted it was good for his company. Working alongside the airport company, they found many efficiencies and savings. As a result they became more competitive and were able to bring these efficiencies to other clients.

Enforcing a 20% cost cut just because you can is macho but dumb. On the other hand, *helping* your supplier find ways to reduce costs by 20% is very clever.

Problem-solving techniques

There are many problem-solving techniques and you may have your own favourite.

At its very simplest, it involves asking three questions:

1.   Where are you now?
2.   Where do you want to be?
3.   How do you get from where you are now to where you want to be?

The answer to the first question comes from each party sharing their current situation along with any problems they are facing and constraints they may have.

The answer to the second question is the win-win: you want to get to a place where both parties have their win, both parties achieve their interests.

And the third answer is the practical plan of action that takes you from your current situation to your desired outcome.

Easy, eh?

And sometimes it is easy. Get specific, the more specific you are, the more likely the answer will just fall out. Be very clear about your current situation, be very clear about where you want to get, put the two descriptions side by side and compare them. If you are specific enough, your plan of action will be very apparent.

The genius of Walt Disney

Walt Disney was not only a creative genius but also a business genius. On three occasions (short animations, feature film animations and entertainment theme parks), he revolutionised an industry or built a whole new one. He created "wins" like few other people have done. Today, 40 years after his death, his company makes sales of $35 billion each year.

He developed his own approach to problem-solving that underlay his success. As modelled by Robert Dilts, he believed it required three very different stages and each stage needed different thinking.

"There were actually three different Walts: the dreamer, the realist, and the spoiler. You never knew which one was coming into your meeting." So said Disney's colleagues, Ollie Johnstone and Frank Thomas in their book, The Illusion of Life: Disney Animation. And from this, Dilts identified the three different stages of problem-solving.

The first stage was the 'Dreamer' phase, where the vision was given its space to expand and become a dream. It was important to start by really giving it its wings, allowing the thinking to go beyond the norms of current possibility. Thinking along the lines of:

- 'Wouldn't it be great if...'
- 'What I would love to see would be...'
- 'If we knew we couldn't fail...'
- 'If we had unlimited budget...'
- 'If we could go for an impossible solution...'

Of course, some people reading these, would just think they are ridiculous, they are impossible. And that was exactly Walt Disney's point. At this stage, they are impossible because he wanted to break free of a lot of the constraints that hold people's thinking back.

Walt Disney was very practical – $35 billion a year is exceedingly practical – but he felt it important that, at the first stage, people's ideas should not be held back by considerations of possibility.

It was in the second stage that the thinking becomes practical. In this stage, the 'Realist' stage, you ask "what do you need to do to be able to bring that dream about into reality?" This is the planning stage. This is where you get realistic and consider real-world issues and build a step-by-step plan of action.

And then the third stage is even more practical. It is called the 'Critic' phase, where you go beyond being practical and allow yourself to be cynical. Look at your realistic plan and consider what are all of the things that might go wrong. This thinking enables you to catch all the pitfalls and develop a water-tight plan of action.

If you want to see the power of such thinking, look at the Apollo Project. When Kennedy announced his support, in 1961, for a manned moon landing it was a pipe-dream. Most people had never entertained the thought, it was so far from the realms of possibility. Even most experts considered it impossible given the huge technological leaps that would need to be made. And yet, by planning step-by-step what was required to be done, the 'impossible' was made possible within the decade. To quote Jim Lovell on Neil Armstrong's landing, 'It's not a miracle, we just decided to do it".

Walt Disney recognised for this three-stage approach to be successful, it was necessary to ring-fence the three different thinking styles. He set aside separate rooms in his headquarters where team members could only dream; where, no dream could be too extraordinary. He dedicated other rooms, where you were only allowed to be realistic. And other rooms still where the critics were given the space to question what was missing, or what needed to change.

He realised that by isolating the different parts, it was possible to avoid such scenarios as the dreamers starting to dream, only to be shot down by the critics. Or the realists being chastised by the dreamers for being too pedestrian or unimaginative. Each mode of thinking has its part to play but each must be listened to by itself.

This combination of creative and pragmatic, positive and realistic, is very powerful. Apply it to your negotiation and you will generate a solution that will really create extra value for all parties, a solution that will incentivise everybody to work towards it; you will generate a realistic action plan to achieve it; and you will also pre-empt all the possible pitfalls that may prevent its successful implementation.

Be creative

Negotiating is a surprisingly creative process and creative thinking is the key to creating greatest value for all involved.

Always think beyond the obvious and work on the principle that there is likely to be more than one solution for every problem. Some of these solutions will be better than others and which one is best can only be determined through analysis.

In Neil Rackham's studies, he found that on average the top negotiators generated 5.1 options per issue, against the 2.6 options thought of by others.

In fact, creativity is a critical skill in business in general. It is core to all progress. The magazine Business Week celebrated its 75th anniversary with a special edition dedicated entirely to it because it believed the previous 75 years of growth we had enjoyed were all driven by innovation.

So how do we be more creative? Linus Pauling, twice Nobel Prize winner, was asked how he had so many great ideas. "If you want to have good ideas", he said, "you must have many ideas. Most of them will be wrong, and what you have to learn is which ones to throw away." This is creativity in a nutshell: have lots of ideas and throw away the bad ones.

In a negotiation, the first thing is not to accept the first solution presented as the only one. It can be introduced as "Well, the obvious solution would be to...but perhaps before we jump straight into that, I wonder whether we could think of any others?".

Alternatively, if someone else suggests the first solution, it can be greeted with "Yes, that's a very good solution and would be quite feasible. Let's try to think of a few more possibilities before we decide on our approach".

Of course, even though it was a process that won Linus Pauling two Nobel Prizes, many business people are not as enlightened as him and you may lose credibility by pouring out lots of ideas in a meeting, without due consideration of quality. Worse, in a negotiation, they may hold you to them as part of the agreement!

So, you may wish to introduce the concept with phrases such as:

- Let's do a bit of brainstorming...
- Let's consider some different possibilities...
- What if we were to be a bit more creative...

If they are not open to this, then you can still do the brainstorming outside of the negotiation, either with your own team, by yourself or with someone you have roped in for the purpose. Then when you introduce any idea, you may wish to signal that it is from a brainstorm and is not necessarily to be taken seriously by introducing it with phrases such as:

- I'm not saying this is what we go for...
- One option might be to...
- What if we were to...
- In an ideal world...

It is essential that everyone understands that at this stage there is no commitment to any specific idea mentioned.

Radical thinking

Breakthroughs come from questioning everything: what are you assuming that may not need to be the case?

1968 was the year of revolutions. Political revolutions swept through the world. It even saw a revolution in the world of athletics. Throughout its history, the high jump would be performed with either the scissors kick or the straddle jump. Had anyone suggested a jumper should jump head first and backwards, they would have been laughed out of town. At the Mexico Olympics, Dick Fosbury tried it and won the gold medal, setting a new record. Nowadays, few serious athletes use any other method.

Similarly, in the 1950's, Parry O'Brien, a shot-putter, questioned the historical technique of rocking backwards and forwards before throwing. Could he throw further with a different method? He invented a way to gain extra momentum by swivelling his body around 180 degrees before launching the put and, in doing so, broke the world record 17 times and won 116 consecutive competitions.

To be creative, we have to go beyond our normal thinking patterns. One way of doing this is to deliberately get things wrong. Our normal thinking patterns try very hard, for obvious reasons, to get things right but as a result they tend to come up with normal ideas. If you try to solve a problem using the same thinking patterns, you will tend to end up with the same answers. Deliberately getting the answer wrong will take you to a different place. It can then trigger off a new idea that you would not have thought of otherwise.

In the business world, there are many highly lucrative examples of getting things wrong. Take Viagra: it's working

mechanism is that it enhances the effectivity of nitric oxide (as opposed to nitrous oxide, commonly known as laughing gas. Taking laughing gas will probably have the opposite effect of Viagra. Your partner taking laughing gas will definitely have the opposite effect of Viagra) and was originally seen as likely to be highly effective for lowering blood pressure. Tests had gone very well and human trials were now being conducted. Unfortunately, they did not seem to be producing the results expected and no significant benefits were being seen compared to the controls. So the project was cancelled and the drugs were recalled.

Except some of the participants of the trial held on to their supply of drugs. In accordance with procedure, the researchers asked again for them to be sent back and, again, the participants refused.

Eventually, the researchers enquired exactly why the participants were holding on to them and they were told of some of the more gravity-defying side-effects of the drug. A sexual revolution was born.

 Action points

Reframe the negotiation as a problem to be solved in partnership with your counterparty:

▸ Start by agreeing on any procedural aspects of the negotiation, easily agreed upfront, before anything of substance is discussed. Then, once established, they can be referred back to during any sticking point and help smooth the proceedings

▸ Establish the bigger picture drivers for all parties

▸ Ask how you can help them achieve theirs and how they can help you achieve yours

▸ Be creative *and* realistic

▸ Be tough on the problem, not on the person.

8.2 COMMUNICATION

Intrinsic to this stage and, indeed, all negotiation is communication. The quality of the solution depends upon the quality of the communication. Accordingly, we will take time here to see how we can improve our communication skills so we can become a better negotiator and get better deals.

It is such a deeply embedded process in all human interaction that we take it for granted. As George Bernard Shaw pointed out, "The problem with communication ... is the *illusion* that it has been accomplished". We assume it is a straightforward process and that when we say something, the other party understands us fully and we, of course, understand them perfectly as well.

It ain't necessarily so. It can be mis-hearings (did Madonna really sing "Like a virgin, touched for the thirty-first time"?) or misunderstandings but either way the message received is not always the same as the message sent. We need to stop taking communication for granted and learn how to do it better.

Now, some of the more hard-nosed, practical sorts amongst you might be thinking: "Communication? I know how to communicate, I was born talking. Let's drop the fluffy, psychological stuff and let's learn how to negotiate".

We are. If you want to get the best deal out there, the deal you did not even know existed; if you want to find out the information the other guy is trying to hide from you; if you want to make sure that the deal you thought you agreed is what gets delivered in practice; then this section is for you.

Be responsible for the success of the communication

If it is such a mine-field, who is responsible for ensuring the success of the communication? Is it the speaker or the listener?

The answer is that *both* parties are *100%* responsible. Note: this is not the same as 50/50. Both parties are 100% wholly, individually responsible.

So if I am trying to get a message across to you, it is down to me to make sure that I express my message in a way that you understand me fully. And I have to check that you understand and if I suspect you have not fully grasped it, I need to think of another way to say it until you do.

Likewise, if someone is telling me something, and that information will help me, well then it is up to me to make sure that I get the information and that I check that what I have got is what they meant.

Of course, it all depends upon how important the communication is to me. If I am not interested in the success of the negotiation, then it does not matter. But if I want the deal, and I want to get a good deal, I should take responsibility for it. If the deal breaks down, it is no help that I can blame the other person for being a poor communicator, I am still left without a deal.

Where does communication go wrong?

The simplest model of communication is that one person has an idea, verbalises it, the other person hears it and understands it.

The aim of good communication is to minimise the gap between the two understandings, the gap between the two thought bubbles in the picture. It is the gap between these thought bubbles that causes so many problems in negotiations and their implementation.

There is plenty of potential for error. In fact, at each of the stages in this picture there are possibilities for things to go wrong. If we take *this* as our starting point for communication, we will likely be more successful.

Getting your message across successfully

If the other person is talking, there are powerful methods we can use to make sure we fully understand what they are saying and, indeed, not saying. But firstly, let us look how we can ensure we successfully navigate the communication minefield.

- **Thought does not mean said**

The key here is simply to be conscious of your communication. Rather than babbling away without really thinking about what you are saying:

- pause
- collect your thoughts
- ask yourself what are you really trying to get across
- then, as you say it, mentally check was that what you actually intended to communicate.

- **Said does not mean heard**

Be assertive! Talk loudly and clearly and articulate every syllable. Do not talk over people, they will not hear what you say if they are talking themselves.

But there is more to it than this, be interesting too! They may well be able to hear you but do you still have their attention or have they switched off and started thinking about tonight's dinner or last night's television?

To make it easier for them to stay attentive: do not talk too fast or too slow, do not talk for too long, use short and simple words, use words they understand and put it in terms of the benefit for them.

- **Heard does not mean understood**

This is not dissimilar – use short and simple words, use their language and put the message across in terms of their world. Do not use jargon or acronyms they will not understand.

Check they have understood you. A direct question such as "Do you understand?" will nearly always get the answer "Yes", so it is better to ask an open question such as "What do you understand by this?".

Alternatively, an effective indirect approach is to ask them about something that is *implied* from what you have said and gauge their understanding by the nature of their response.

Going visual can help. Draw it as well as say it, this can convey complicated thoughts very simply and it gives the other person a tangible reference point to clarify anything they still do not fully understand. Even writing on a flipchart or a piece of paper gives something to point to which can help.

- **Understood does not mean agreed**

This one is simple – check. Ask them if they agree. Again, the direct question will nearly always get the answer "Yes" so this is not enough. Check from the non-verbal communication that the agreement is full. Do the body language, the facial expression, the tone of voice suggest otherwise? Again, it can be effective to ask a different question: ask what specifically they are agreeing to, or ask indirectly about something that is implied by the agreement, and gauge their response.

If you suspect that they are not fully in agreement, despite their "Yes", ask them what else is missing or what else it might need for them to be completely behind it.

- **Agreed does not mean applied**

This is the most important aspect of the negotiation, that what is agreed actually gets implemented. Just because you have a signature does not mean it will happen in real-life.

To ensure this, the other party needs to be incentivised so the agreement needs to be win-win. Again, check. Monitor that the agreement is actually applied. As we will see in the next chapter, "Trust but verify".

- **Applied does not mean maintained.**

Try to get the agreement locked-in, as well, so that as the world changes and different scenarios unfold, parties are still incentivised to apply the agreement. Try to consider as many of these scenarios as possible and include them in the agreement.

The simple rule is that for each of these stages, beforehand be conscious of the scope for error and afterwards check that it was as successful as possible.

The wonders of communication

As an aside, let us take a short moment to look at exactly what does go on in the communication process and see what an amazing phenomenon it really is. Let us say we are chatting away and I say to you "David Beckham likes chocolate cupcakes" and you nod knowingly and say "Yep, I bet he does". What is going on?

Well, firstly, the neurons in my brain configure themselves in such a way as to represent David Beckham. Now, I have never met the guy, he may well be in a different continent as we speak, and I have certainly never seen him eat chocolate cupcakes.

But somehow my brain moves chemicals around and fires electrical stimuli in such a way that I get a picture of him in my head and I can see him eating a cupcake and I get a sense of him enjoying it.

That, even as the first step, is quite phenomenal that my brain can do that through chemicals and electrical impulses. But what happens next?

Next, those same neurons make my mouth and vocal chords move in such a way that as I breathe, it moves the air in a particular way to make a particular sound. But what do I mean by "particular sound"? A sound is simply changes in air pressure. Now, your ear then feels those changes in air pressure. And it separates out all of the random changes in air pressure due to the wind or a door closing, and it separates out the changes in air pressure due to the radio on in the background or the other person in the room talking on the phone, and it "tunes into" the particular changes in air pressure that were made by me when I spoke; when my vocal chords moved in that way as directed by the electrical impulses from my neurons.

Even as I write this, I find it incredible!

And then the third stage is simply gob-smacking: your brain converts the air pressure changes felt by the ear into electrical

impulses which re-configure the neurons in *your* brain in such a way that you get a picture in your mind of David Beckham eating chocolate cupcakes. This is nothing short of miraculous!

I suppose we should not be surprised, evolution spent 3.5 billion years perfecting it. But we take it all for granted and when you see the astonishing processes that are actually taking place is there really any wonder that communication can go wrong?

Listening

When people think of good communicators, they think of people who are good at talking. Talking is actually third on the list of key skills for good communication, listening and questioning both trump telling.

But as the receiver of the message, similar caveats apply: it is dangerous to assume they have articulated their exact thoughts, it is dangerous to assume you have fully grasped their meaning, it is dangerous to assume any of the stages have transpired hitch-free.

Key to receiving their message as intended is to listen and to listen well. And there is good and bad news about listening.

The bad news is that it is actually quite difficult to do and we are generally pretty poor at it. Too often, we stop listening to the other person because we think we know what they are going to say or we are focussing on what we will say next and how wonderful it will sound. Just as frequently we are thinking about lunch or last night's television. Thus projects over-run, sales are lost and marriages end in divorce.

The good news, however, is that we can learn to listen better and if we do, we stand out! Because everyone else is so bad at it, if we listen well we have a competitive advantage – people tend to think we are nice and that we are intelligent. Such a large return on such a small investment.

How to listen well

The key to listening well is active listening. Active listening involves:
- focus
- asking questions and engaging with what they are saying
- listening for the meaning behind the words and for what is not actually said
- listening to the non-verbal communication
- listening to the sub-text and the emotion
- checking your understanding is correct.

It is a natural thing for our minds to wander when someone else is talking for any extended period of time (with some people it is almost essential!). The key is to notice when this happens and, when you do, bring your attention back to what they are saying. Keep doing this and you will train your mind to stay focussed for longer and longer periods of time.

Engaging with what they are saying is very important. The good news is that, surprisingly, if you *pretend* you are interested, you soon *become* interested. Ask questions about what they are saying and you will actually generate an engagement with it which will, in turn, make it easier for you to listen.

As you listen, listen for the full meaning of their words beyond the simple dictionary definitions.

Professor Schultz Von Thun of Hamburg University invented a model called The Four Sides of Communication (sometimes called The Four Ears model) in which he described how each message has four levels to it: factual, self-revelation, relationship, appeal to action.

- **Factual**

The factual level conveys the pure facts of the matter at hand. In the illustration below when the man says the lights are green, the factual content is simply that the traffic lights are green, as opposed to any other colour.

- **Self-revelation**

This aspect reveals information about the person who is making the communication. We cannot fail to reveal something about our self each time we talk, it is a leak we cannot plug. When the man says the lights are green, he may well be communicating that he is in a hurry or that he is an impatient person.

- **Relationship**

This level of the communication reveals information about the relationship between the sender and the receiver. In the example below, the man may well be annoyed with the driver or think she is a bad driver or a slow driver or that he is always late for things because of her.

- **Appeal to action**

Finally, there is the appeal to action. Below, it is likely to be "Come on, drive!".

If a communication carries four levels of information, we can choose which one we respond to. Notice to which level the woman below responds. In replying "Are you driving or am I?", she is almost certainly replying to the relationship level. Her response, too, has four levels of information – and we can easily guess what the appeal to action is!

In active listening, we listen out for all four levels of information. It is not always that all four will be important but it could be any one of them and not simply the factual level.

A key element to listen out for is the emotional component. Emotions are very powerful forces in negotiating and it is important you pick up on these. If the communicator seems angry or disappointed or enthusiastic or triumphant or bored or, indeed, conveys any feelings, this is very useful information for your negotiation stance. The words alone may not suggest any emotion, you have to look behind them at the non-verbal signals like the tone of voice, the facial expression or other body language.

What is more, if you notice the emotion and you acknowledge it, it is a very powerful way of showing that you have listened and taken on board what they are saying. If you say "I hear that you're disappointed about the price, you thought it would be a lot lower, let me explain how we arrived at it", they are much more likely to be receptive.

Finally, showing that you have listened to them, by summarising what they have said, checking and clarifying your understanding and, if necessary, acknowledging their feelings is a very powerful method of building the other person's trust in you. If someone feels really listened to, they will engage more wholly in the dialogue and will be more willing to make concessions themselves.

Asking the right question

We have just seen that the most important is listening.

The second most important skill is the ability to ask questions. The right questions will give you the information you need to know; and this, even if the other party does not necessarily want to reveal it. The right question can be used to clarify misunderstandings as well and, as we have already seen, they can even be used to influence and encourage the other party to come to a deal.

Referring back to our model above, how do we know they have articulated what they meant? Indeed, how do we even know they have thought through the situation fully themselves? How do we know we have understood exactly what they meant?

By asking the right question.

Uncovering the unknown unknowns

To succeed in negotiations, you must know as many of the facts of the situation as possible.

Not everything is knowable. We may guess future economic conditions, we may forecast future sales, we may estimate the costs of the operations, but we cannot know them for certain because, simply, not everything is knowable.

Donald Rumsfeld, the former U.S. Secretary of Defence, was lampooned for talking about unknown unknowns but he was right. It is the unknown unknowns that can be crucial in the success or failure of a negotiation.

Known unknowns are straightforward, we can usually prepare and find out what we need to know from an appropriate source. But it is the things that we do not even know we do not know that can catch us out.

A classic example of such a "black swan" event (see "The Black Swan" by Nassim Nicholas Taleb) was the tragic attack on the World Trade Centre in September 11th, 2001. It was unpredictable and so no one could have included its impact in any deal negotiated at the time. And yet its impact was felt massively across the world.

But, as Taleb points out, black swan events depend on the observer. What is a black swan to one person, may be common knowledge to another. He tells the story of a turkey that is fed well for a thousand days by a butcher. Every day for a thousand days confirms what the turkey already knows, that he is well loved by his butcher, and every day the turkey gets fatter and fatter. Then, one Thanksgiving Day, the turkey gets a surprise...which was, of course, no surprise to the butcher.

Your negotiation counterparty may know the information but does not tell you. Maliciously? Maybe, but more often because they assume you know already. Or think they did tell you. Or they did not see its relevance. Remember – thought does not mean said...

Find what the other party does not want you to know

How do you make sure you are not the turkey and the party with whom you are negotiating is not the butcher?

In 1981, Microsoft negotiated a deal with Seattle Computer Products to license their operating system, known as 86-DOS. The deal was $10,000 up-front plus $15,000 for each sub-license sold by Microsoft. As such, Microsoft paid a total of $25,000 because they only ever sub-licensed it to one customer.

Seattle Computer Products were not told the name of this customer and, shortly afterwards, Microsoft offered an extra $50,000 to buy the product outright. It was agreed.

Seattle Computer Products did not know one crucial fact: the name of the company that Microsoft were going to sub-license the operating system to. Consequently, they did not know the enormous value of their product.

The unnamed customer turned out to be IBM who launched the new PC using the re-branded MS-DOS as the operating system. In the next 10 years, Microsoft earnt over $200 million from the sales of MS-DOS.

The Questioning Funnel

A quick recap of where we are: we have persuaded the other players in the deal to work together in partnership to find a win-win outcome and we have re-framed the negotiation as a problem to be resolved. We have a good idea of our side of the situation already, what we need to know as thoroughly as possible is their side. These are the unknown unknowns we need to unearth. How do you find out this information which could turn out to be so crucial and yet, at the beginning of the dialogue, you may not even know you do not know?

The answer is a technique known as the Questioning Funnel. It is a technique known well to journalists who want to find out about a story but they do not even know what the story might be; it is known to police detectives who need to find out information but they are not even sure what information they need to find out; it is known to management consultants, to spies, to lawyers and barristers, it is known to anyone who needs information but who does not know even where to start.

In summary, the Questioning Funnel starts very broadly then narrows down as it finds things of interest, things you want to find out more about. It does this by using open and closed questions appropriately, and by starting off with letting the other party set the agenda in terms of the discussion but then slowly guiding it where you want it to go.

Closed Questions	Open Questions
Did you like the film last night?	What did you like about the film last night?
Is business going well?	How is business going at the moment?

As many of you will know, if we take the questions on the left hand column, the answers to these are likely to be short, one word answers – either "yes" or "no". This is not necessarily that helpful if you are exploring and wanting to dig up some useful information.

The questions on the right, however, leave a lot more room for the other person to answer at length.

Step 1 – Open indirect questions:

The Questioning Funnel starts with open, direct questions. They are open so it allows for a more expansive answer and they are indirect so it is the other person that sets the agenda. After all, they are privy to the information so let them talk about it. It might well be a straightforward question like "How is business?" or "So tell me, what is your view on the new project?". These will then allow the other person to answer the question at length, talking about whatever they happen to know about it.

Step 2 – Open direct questions:

As they answer the question, it may be they mention something that you think could be of interest. So the second step in the Questioning Funnel is to guide them in this direction by asking open, direct questions. For example, they may mention some problems on the project and you may want to find out more so you ask, "What are those problems you referred to? What impact are they having?". Again, the question is open which allows them to answer at length, but you have directed them to the area you wish to find out about. You are now setting the agenda of the conversation.

Step 3 – Probing questions:

Even as you guide them to what you would like to know about, there will naturally be gaps in their answer which you would like to fill in. These may be things they did not consider relevant, or they assume you know already or maybe they simply forget but you feel it would be useful for you to know.

So step three of the Questioning Funnel is to ask probing questions such as "What exactly do you mean by...?" or "What happened specifically when...?"

Step 4 – Closed directed questions:

Step 4 involves closed, directed questions to make sure your understanding is correct and that there is no room for wriggling. "Did you agree?", "Do you have proof?", "Did they use those exact words?".

Step 5 – Summarising and checking:

Then the final step is to summarise your understanding in your own words and play it back to them, checking you heard and understood correctly.

This is a very powerful way to explore the areas of knowledge that you do not know about and the other party does and for you to zoom in on those areas that you feel would be useful for you to know more. In the course of the conversation, you may move up and down this funnel several times as you uncover different areas of importance.

As a method of finding out the things that you don't know you don't know, it is very useful. And as a way to bridge that communication gap, the gap between the two thought bubbles in our picture at the beginning of this section, it is very effective.

QUESTIONING FUNNEL

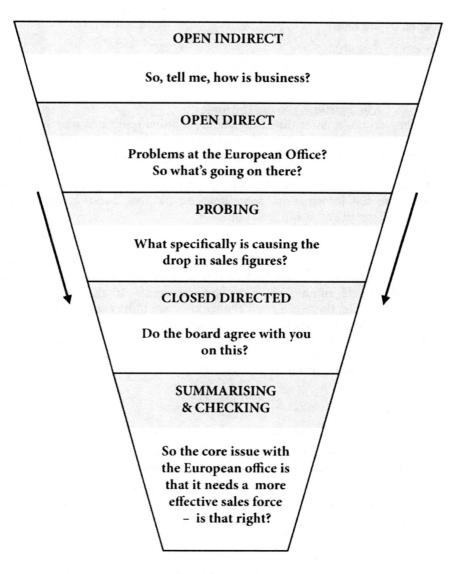

OPEN INDIRECT

So, tell me, how is business?

OPEN DIRECT

Problems at the European Office?
So what's going on there?

PROBING

What specifically is causing the
drop in sales figures?

CLOSED DIRECTED

Do the board agree with you
on this?

**SUMMARISING
& CHECKING**

So the core issue with
the European office is
that it needs a more
effective sales force
– is that right?

Target

Of course, the other party may refuse to tell you the answers. No doubt, Seattle Computer Products asked Microsoft the name of their customer and no doubt Microsoft were coy with their answer. What options are open to you here?

- **Research**

You can research the topic outside of the meeting and you may well be able to find out your information from some other source.

- **Ask questions around the topic**

If they do not answer direct questions, indirect questions may give you answers that will imply the information you are looking for. Often a party is not allowed to divulge certain information for confidentiality reasons but they may be happy for you to know, as long as it does not look that the information has come directly from them. Even if they do not want to give you the information, sometimes an indirect question may catch them off guard and it will leak out.

- **Body language**

Body language is especially important when the other party is trying to hide information. We will look at this in more depth later on, but non-verbal signals often give away information. If they are looking uncomfortable, there is a good chance they are hiding something or they are not telling the full truth. A good tip is to run something past them and gauge their response, especially in the non-verbal signals. For example, casually mention the rumours they are talking to a competitor and gauge the look on their face. It may well speak louder than any words.

Finding out the real situation behind what they are saying

So you follow the Questioning Funnel and you ask lots of questions and you find out exactly what the situation is and now you are fully informed.

Well, unfortunately, it is not quite as simple as that. For a start, as we have seen, they may not tell you the truth or the whole truth. Even if they do answer your questions in good faith and give you lots of information, maybe that is not enough.

If we go back to our communication model, even if you do everything that is in your control and you listen intently and hear everything that is said and you understand everything that is heard, there is one step in the model *before that* which is actually beyond your control. The very first

Simon Horton   186

step in the model – "thought does not mean said" already contains potential for error. And even that thought may not have been accurate in the first place.

Negotiations take place in the real world and so all your questions of the other party will be about real world things. But the communication may not necessarily be an accurate representation of the real world.

Let us take a concrete example. You supply components to a manufacturer and you are re-negotiating the terms of the contract. In order to get a rough idea of the current commercial situation you ask them how business is doing and they reply confidently that sales are up.

Great, now you can negotiate in the knowledge that you will be shipping more components than before and this will obviously impact how the talks proceed.

But wait, what does "sales are up" actually mean in the real world?

Your natural thought is of a graph that probably looks something like this:

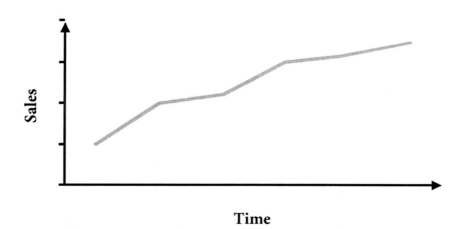

Time

But maybe, when you look at the actual sales figures, the reality is different. Maybe it is more like:

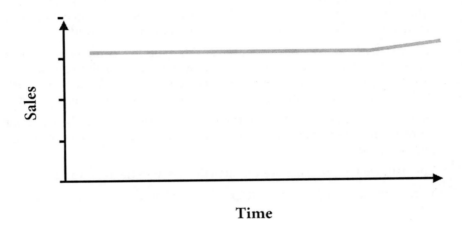

Yes, sales are up but marginally.

Or it could be like:

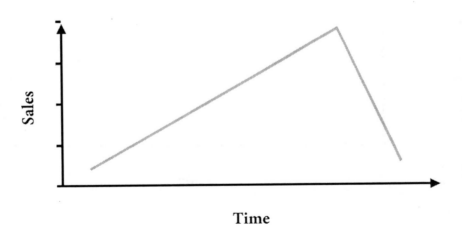

Indeed, sales are up compared to this time last year, but the trend is significantly down.

Or again:

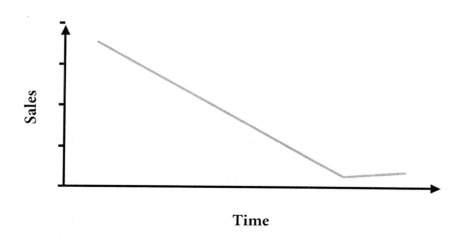

Here, sales are up compared to last month but significantly down compared to last year.

Or maybe sales are up *a lot*, this could be a problem of its own, can you meet the demand?

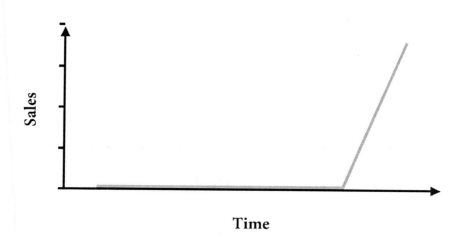

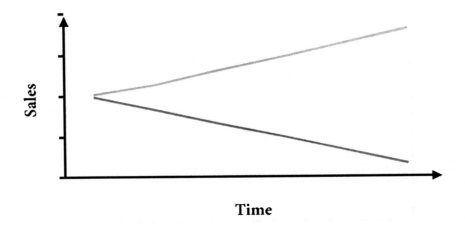

Maybe, when he said sales are up, he was referring to a different product line or a different market or the total sales figures. But, unfortunately, your particular product line and market is on its way down.

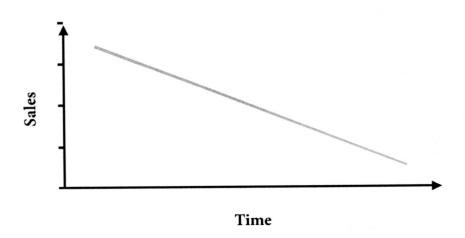

And, finally, maybe the sales are actually unequivocally *down*, but he got his facts wrong or he was told they were up or he misunderstood what he had been told. Chinese whispers is a game that is frequently played in business without the participants necessarily knowing!

So many ways for such a simple communication, said in good faith, to be misleading. Sign your deal on the basis of any of these incorrect interpretations and you have signed up for a bum deal.

How do you find out what is the reality that lies behind the words?

Get Specific

The answer is to get specific. Specifically, use the word "specifically".

- "Which sales specifically are up?"
- "How much up are they, specifically?"
- "Compared to when, specifically?"

"Specifically" is an extremely powerful word, it enables the conversation to telescope in to the necessary level of detail. "Sales are up" hides so many possible real-world scenarios, "specifically" digs out the true situation.

And details can be important, they can mean the difference between deal or no-deal. Imagine the following conversation:

Customer: "The project *has* to be completed by the end of May, it's when we go live. The date is on all our marketing material, it can't be moved"

Supplier: "I'm afraid it is going to be impossible to complete it all in that time-frame. We simply don't have the resources."

Let us freeze-frame here. Currently, there is no deal. The customer has to have the project completed by the end of May, the supplier cannot deliver. Ok, now let us resume the conversation.

Supplier: "Tell me, which specific parts of the project need to be finished by then and are there any bits that can be delivered later?"

Customer: "Well, the client interface obviously, and the data capture element. But it's true, the management reporting can be delivered after".

Supplier: "Ok, that is feasible then. We can deliver."

Zooming into the detail and looking at the specific deliverables, we are able to reach a deal.

Of course, there are other words you can use too, and I would recommend you do, unless you really want to annoy the other party. Instead of always using the word "specifically", you can vary and use:

- precisely
- particularly
- in particular
- exactly
- what do you mean by...?
- if we can get into the detail...
- to remove ambiguity...
- in concrete terms...

There are many different ways of doing it but the main thing is to get specific.

Being Economical With The Truth

Being "economical with the truth" is a very common negotiation tactic.

In 1985, Peter Wright, a former Assistant Director at MI5, tried to publish his memoirs "Spycatcher" which detailed many practices by the UK secret services, including plots against the British Prime Minister, Harold Wilson, and plots to assassinate President Nasser of Egypt.

The British government tried to prevent its publication and, in a high-profile trial that really caught the public imagination at the time, the Cabinet Secretary Robert Armstrong was found to have misled the court. In his defence, he said he did not lie but had been, famously, "economical with the truth". That is, he had presented some facts that were true but had deliberately withheld other highly important facts that would have conveyed a whole other meaning.

Who knows, maybe Microsoft said to Seattle Computer Products "We only want to licence it to one client". That would have been totally true and it would convey the situation in a particular way (a way that you might think "poor little Microsoft"). That one client was IBM, of course, and they probably forgot to mention it. Had they done so, it would convey the situation in a wholly different manner (not poor little Microsoft, at all!).

It is not lying, it is holding back certain facts in order to present the situation in a particular light.

- We only have one client *(who happens to be IBM)*
- It is just a small piece of land *(but seismography charts suggest there is oil underneath)*
- The defendant admits he did lose his temper *(actually, he ran amok with a machete)*

The way to counteract this tactic, again, is to get specific.

- "Who specifically is the client?"
- "What specifically interests you about this piece of land?"
- "You say he lost his temper, what did he do specifically?"

Interestingly, people are loath to lie. Most people do see a moral difference between lying and being economical with the truth. Many people are comfortable holding back certain facts (even if they know this will mislead) but are uncomfortable actively lying.

If you notice any squirming as you ask your questions, you are probably getting close to something of interest – something they do not want to lie about, but nor do they want to tell the whole truth. In this case, keep digging!

Backtracking

In making sure our communication is successful, it is useful to backtrack on a regular basis. By backtracking, we mean summarising what has been said so far and checking everyone's understanding and agreement.

Play back to the other party what you have heard to make sure you have understood them correctly; get them to play back to you what they have heard to make sure they have understood you. At certain points in the conversation, do a quick summary: "Before we go on, just to make sure we all agree on this point, what we are saying is…"

In meetings, there is often an individual who listens, checks for full understanding and summarises where the meeting has got to. Studies have actually shown that this person is often viewed as the most influential person in that meeting. They have not necessarily contributed much but they have listened, clarified and summarised. This seems quite a simple way to be seen as influential and help shape a negotiation the way you would like it go.

Other studies by Neil Rackham, the inventor of the SPIN sales methodology, also found that skilled negotiators tested understanding and summarised proceedings more than twice as much as average ones.

Dealing with Chinese whispers

"Send reinforcements, we are going to advance," said the front-line battalion. "Send three and fourpence, we are going to a dance," heard the HQ at the other end of the crackling telephone line and, ever-helpful, duly obliged.

We have seen how complicated is the real underlying process of communication and therefore the high chances of it going wrong. And that is in a very simple one-to-one communication. How much greater chance, then, of error when the communication involves different stages as the message is passed down the line between people.

Organisations are so big these days that information gets passed from one person to another and, unfortunately, as we have seen already, Chinese whispers is a game that is often played without the participants knowing. Information comes second- or third-hand, data becomes out of date, people make commitments that are beyond their authority to deliver.

In the siege of the Iranian embassy in London in 1979, the police negotiator brought in a translator at the request of one of the gunmen. This turned out to be a mistake because the translator said many things they had not been authorised or told to say. Quite against orders, for example, he told the kidnappers that they were all going to die. This is unlikely to happen in any of your negotiations (I am guessing) but rogue communications may still need to be managed.

The answer is always to get as close to the source of information as possible. Do not trust a second- or third-hand report. Be polite as possible but ask to see the evidence or the source material.

Anthony Bolton, the legendary fund manager, generally eschewed a company's financial reports when picking which stocks to invest in. His view was that published accounts were generally meaningless – after all, how meaningful were Enron's or WorldCom's? At best, they describe the past and an investor wants to know the future. So, instead, he would prefer to park his car for a week outside the gates of the company's factory and he would count the number of lorries going in and out. That was raw data and it was current and as such much more meaningful than anything published in last year's accounts.

 **Action points**

Reframe the negotiation as a problem to be solved in partnership with your counterparty:

▸ Start by agreeing on any procedural aspects of the negotiation. These are often easily agreed upfront, before anything of substance is discussed, and then, once established, can be referred back to any sticking point and help smooth the proceedings

▸ Establish the bigger picture drivers for all parties

▸ Ask how you can help them achieve theirs and how they can help you achieve yours

▸ Be creative *and* realistic

▸ Be tough on the problem, not on the person.

8.3 DEADLOCK

Expect deadlock

One of the tougher situations to crack in a negotiation is when there seems to be a deadlock due to mutually exclusive demands. These arise frequently and can sink a deal. The good news is that in most cases they do not need to, in most cases a solution exists.

Expect deadlock. Of *course* there will be deadlock, that is exactly why you are negotiating. Expect a stand-off. Expect a time when there seems to be no way forward. Expect a time when their demand seems to be unavoidably at the expense of yours. This is not the end of the negotiation. This is just part of the process. Take your time, carry on the conversation, be creative, you will find a way through.

Or, of course, not. Maybe you will not find a way and the deal fails. *You need to be ok with this scenario*. At all times in any negotiation you need to have sufficiently good alternatives that you are comfortable if the deal does not succeed. Otherwise you will make too many concessions and the deal will not be worthwhile.

So, with that proviso, how can we resolve apparent deadlocks?

Deadlocks occur within the positional bargaining approach. If one party insists on certain outcomes from the negotiation, and so does the other, there is a chance that these will be mutually exclusive. The insistence on them will cause an impasse in the negotiations.

They occur if both parties want exactly the same thing, and there is only one of it and it is indivisible. Or they occur if there is no "area of agreement":

Let us saying I am selling a property and I would like between £380k and £440k. The prospective buyer is looking for something over £350k but has a maximum budget of £420k. The deal looks like this:

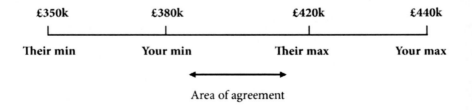

Area of agreement

However, if the maximum they could afford to pay is £390k and the minimum you would accept is £410k, there is no area of agreement and the deal looks like this:

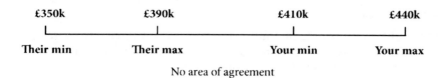

| £350k | £390k | £410k | £440k |
| Their min | Their max | Your min | Your max |

No area of agreement

Sticking with positions and, in particular, using the sole dimension of price there is a stalemate. Fortunately, there are many ways to get around such mutually exclusive deadlocks, some of which we have met already.

Keeping rapport whilst sticking to your guns

Firstly, let us stress how important it is to maintain rapport whilst discussing the tougher issues and this does not mean giving in any way. One of the four key principles from Fisher and Ury's "Getting to Yes" is 'Separate the person from the problem'. That is, be rapportful with the person but be tough on the problem.

One body language trick that helps with this is to stand or sit at 45 degrees to the other person. If you are directly opposite each other, that can be confrontational, but shifting 45 degrees deflects this.

Then have the sticking point written down on a piece of paper (for example, it could be a report or an email or a contract or simply the two disparate prices, as above) and have it slightly away from the two of you, not directly in between. This 'objectifies' the problem and makes it separate from the relationship. Whenever you talk about the problem, look at the piece of the paper. Whenever you talk about the solution or the relationship, look back at your counterparty.

This is a way to make sure that the relationship does not get contaminated with the problem. It does not have to be a piece of paper, it can be a laptop or anything else physical that can be linked to the issue. The important thing is that this is where you look whenever you talk about the difficult stuff; whenever you talk about good things, look back at the person. It is a simple trick and it helps.

Get back to the bigger picture

Often the simplest way to get around a sticking point is to get back to basics: remind yourselves of why you are here and what you are trying to achieve. When you focus on the bigger picture, it gives you more flexibility in achieving a deal.

The traditional example that illustrates this is the orange. Let us imagine, there is one orange and you want it and I want it. There is a stand-off. We both stare at it, time slows down, tumbleweed drifts past.

We could fight for it and one of us would win, one of us would lose out. If we have read a negotiations book recently we could agree to compromise and cut it in half – we would each get one half of the orange. But then neither of us would be fully getting what we wanted.

But let us imagine we had just read a negotiation *mastery* book and we knew to focus on the bigger picture. We would ask each other what exactly did we want the orange for? What was the bigger goal that getting the orange would help us achieve?

And it may be that you wanted to make a juice from it and I wanted to bake a cake and needed the zest from the rind. Now, after finding the bigger goals behind the positions, we are both able to get what we want – you get the juice, I get the rind.

Or take the property example above. If I ask the buyer why do they want to buy the property it may well be that they are planning to move to this city in six months time and they saw this on the market and fell in love with it. However, they really can only get finance for £390k. In that case, it may suit all parties if the price of £390k is accepted but they allow me to continue living in it rent-free for those six months.

Address the Real Reason

The stand-off can sometimes be for a reason that is not actually made explicit. Progress, in such an instance, will only be made if the real reason is addressed, even though it is not out in the open. Remember Morgan's maxim, "People buy for very good reasons. And then there is the real reason".

Uncover the underlying sticking point and then it can be resolved.

Be Specific About The Details

What may look like an impasse may not actually turn out to be so when you get into the specifics of the deal.

If we take the orange example, at the detail level, what do I specifically want? I want the rind of the orange. What do you specifically want? You want the juice of the orange. So, although we both said we wanted the orange, in actual fact, what we really wanted were two different things, so there is no deadlock at all.

This is the beauty of that word "specifically" again. What do you want specifically? Why do you need it specifically? What specific part (of the orange) do you actually need? (Of course, they may look at you strangely, "I need the orange part of the orange, specifically", but in most real-life cases it is worth asking).

Again, the property example, where I will accept £410k minimum but the prospective buyer can only afford £390k. When we get into the details of why they cannot afford any more, it may simply be that their mortgage company will not lend them it. This could open up a channel for finding alternative sources of funding for that last £20k and, again, there is a deal now possible.

What else can you bring to the table?

If there is an impasse, think about what else you can bring to the table that has not already been discussed. It is seeing where there are creative possibilities that may break the deadlock.

With the orange, I may have an apple which I can give you for your juice so that I can take the orange for my cake. Or you may have already baked a cake which you are happy to give me so that you can take the orange for your juice.

In the property example there are many possible creative solutions that could be applicable, depending on the realities of the situation. If I was moving out of the area but still working nearby, I could keep the garage and that might bridge the £20k.

Alternatively, the buyers may have a furniture business or a car dealership at which they could give me £20k worth of credit. Better still, a brewery. When it comes to negotiation, creativity brings success.

Go Neutral

You will have your point of view and you will be quite sure it is fair. You will have your figures and evidence to support it and, no doubt, you will have impeccable reasoning too.

And so will they.

And while you are stuck in your position and they stay stuck in theirs, you are unlikely to progress. Somehow you need to find a neutral perspective.

The first thing to do is to 'go neutral' and instead of negotiating as an adversary, act as a mediator.

Imagine stepping out of your point of view and being a mediator in this very situation. If you had to mediate between these two parties, what would you suggest to each? Step into the 'fly on the wall' situation and look at the two parties 'over there'. What can you see from this perspective?

Invite your counterparty to do the same.

Imagine who would be able to give you good neutral advice and imagine what that advice would be. Robert Tedlow, who wrote "The education of Andy Grove" (Fortune, Dec 2005), described how Intel's president, Andy Grove, once called a crisis meeting with the CEO, Gordon Moore. "If we got kicked out", Grove asked, "and the board brought in a new CEO, what do you think he would do?". Moore replied straight away, "He would get us out of memories". Grove said, "Why shouldn't you and I walk out the door, come back, and do it ourselves?"

Refer to objective standards

Fisher and Ury's principle-centred approach rarely gets into such deadlocks. Their first principle is "Focus on interests, not positions", which is the same as looking at the bigger picture. Their second is "Invent options for mutual gain", which is the same as being creative and we can see how this helps avoid stand-offs. And their third principle is "Refer to objective standards" which is another technique that is effective.

Using objective benchmarks or independent data, means the solution is not based on your opinion or your counterparty's opinion but on neutral reference points.

But working objectively is not restricted to data. You can agree on an objective formula for coming to a solution. If the formula is agreed before its results are known, it will be less contentious and easier to agree to, than an actual figure.

Agree a Fair Process

Or you can agree on an objective process.

You can agree to draw lots! In the UK council elections in Great Yarmouth, May 2010, Conservative candidate Bob Peck and Labour candidate Charlie Marsden both had an identical number of votes. After 4 recounts, they could not break the deadlock. It was decided that each would pick from a pack of playing cards and the one who picked the highest would win. Peck drew a three, Marsden a seven. Labour won the seat.

If there are more variables involved, there are other processes that can be used. Any negotiation that involves more than one variable can be reduced to a simple "take it in turns" procedure (eg, you can insert that clause in the contract if I can remove this one).

There are several variations on these:

- If there are significant differences in the size or value of each turn, this can be accommodated. For example, you have first choice, I have second and third choices.
- The uncontested ones are removed from the list first. For example, both parties choose their 'favourite' item. If these are different – great, we can keep them; if we choose the same item, though, they go into a 'contested' pile. At the end, the contested items are dealt with in a turn-by-turn manner or other such process.
- Divide and choose. I cut the cake, you choose which half you want. In other words, one person groups the different items fairly and then the other party can choose which group they want to keep. This incentivises the first person to group as fairly as possible.
- A more sophisticated approach involves three steps:
    1. Each party ascribes 100 points, say, across the different items according to how much they want each.
    2. The highest 'bid' wins each item.

Simon Horton   201

3. If one party ends up with more than 50 points' worth of items, they are re-allocated until the points distribution is as close to an equitable 50-50 split as possible.

These and other fair allocation procedures are discussed in greater length by Professor of politics, Steven Brams and mathematician Alan Taylor in "The Win-Win Solution" and "Fair Division: From cake-cutting to dispute resolution."

Obviously, these will be more successful if the particular process is chosen *before* you reach the deadlock, otherwise there may be a temptation on each side to favour a process that especially benefits them.

Change the Dynamic

If there really is a stand-off, this can often be alleviated by making a change to the environment or the dynamic of the talks:

• build some rapport by telling a joke or funny story or by talking about the news or the sports
• take a break for a cup of tea and reconvene after a short while
• take a longer break and reconvene at a later date
• let someone else do the talking
• change someone in the team
• change the environment and move to a different venue.

Look to other parties to help break the deadlock

If all of your attempts to be as objective as possible come to nothing, look to another party to find a way to free up the discussion.

-	Involve someone else in the discussion who has the authority to break the deadlock

-	Involve someone who can bring something else to the table that changes the balance and so frees up the talks
-	Use an independent mediator. They will not make a decision for you but will help you come to a fair decision. A good mediator can lower the emotional temperature, as well as uncovering less obvious interests and solutions and suggesting face-saving possibilities.
-	Use an arbitrator. An arbitrator will make a decision for you, having weighed up both sides in an objective manner.

If the problem is the person

Often the deadlock is because of the person and not despite them. Some people are not easy and perhaps that is the very reason they have been employed as the negotiator. If you have used all your emotional intelligence and tried all of the above approaches, get out of the deal.

Before you do this, label what is going on and warn them of what you are about to do. Remind them of the value of the deal on the table, remind them of their Plan B and of your Plan B and this should bring them back to their senses.

If not, vamoose. Plan B, here comes!

 Action points

Deadlock happens, expect it, it is part of the process. Keep rapport at all times as you try to resolve it.

▸ Refer back to the bigger picture, what are the parties really trying to achieve here?

▸ Try to work out the real underlying reason for the deadlock and address this

▸ Get into the detail – maybe at the level of detail there is no conflict

▸ Be objective and be creative.

8.4 CONCESSIONS

So we come to the process that most people see as the negotiation itself. The haggle, the give-and-take. Hopefully, you will have understood from what you have read so far that very often this is not the case. Very often, if the deal is set up correctly, little 'haggling' actually takes place.

It would be unrealistic to assume haggling never takes place, however, but when it does, it does not need to be scary or aggressive. It is still most effectively seen as two partners working alongside each other to find the best mutually beneficial result.

In the old-school arm-wrestling approach to negotiations, it is the need for concessions that can actually lead to the deal breaking down. The reason? Neither side wants to make a concession because they think it implies weakness. I have had one lawyer say to me "If you find yourself negotiating, you've lost already". If there is such a macho attitude on both sides, neither party will make any concession and so you get a Mexican stand-off and no deal. Neither party wins.

Legal concessions

Firstly, it is important to point out that in legal disputes a distinction is made between concessions around rights as opposed to wants. It is the court's role to establish rights and this is done on the basis of the merits of the legal case. In the negotiation outside of the courtroom, the talks should be more on what each party wants, independent of their rights.

Obviously, their rights form a backdrop to what is a fair deal and it will also inform the value of your Plan B, that is, the chances of the court finding in your favour. But the informal negotiations should be around what each party would like to achieve, irrespective of their legal rights.

People expect a concession

If you ever find yourself in Morocco, haggling over a carpet in the souk, you will soon recognise that the bargaining normally follows a script. And you can learn this script and be able to predict where the deal will end up, long before you actually got there.

Of course, if you try to save trouble and time and go straight to this price, it does not work. It is so ingrained that they cannot deviate from it.

It can be like this with some old-school negotiators. You may build great rapport and do some great problem-solving together, working indeed as a partnership, but they will still expect a concession. Whatever your starting price, no matter how logically deduced or independently derived, they will expect you to budge, so deeply ingrained is the habit.

Maybe you can build this into your calculation.

The power of concessions

Making a concession can be very powerful. Cialdini's principle of reciprocity says that most people will return that concession with a concession of their own and often their concession can be even bigger than the one you made.

In one study, they canvassed people on the street, half of whom were asked if they would sign up for a day's voluntary work for charity. One in six people signed up. The other half were asked firstly if they would sign up for a two years commitment to two hours a week voluntary work, and then, once this was refused (in all cases), if they would sign up for a day's voluntary work for charity (ie, the same request as the others). This method got a one in two success rate.

The conclusion? The same request given as a concession was accepted *3 times as often* as when made straight out.

Moreover, the second method had twice as many people actually turn up on the day as the first method.

Of course, if they make a concession for us, we do not automatically have to reciprocate with a concession. We should determine if it was made with the sole intention of getting us to make a concession in return. If so, this is manipulation and should be resisted.

Trading

The simplest form of concession to make is the trade. Whether we are trading spices for gold or concession for concession, the basic principle is the same: it is a swap based on the fact that things have different value to different people. I will give you something that is of low value to me and high value to you, in return for you giving me something of low value to you and high value to me.

This is a painless and mutually beneficial trade, both sides walk away with a smile and more than they had before.

From your preparation and from the earlier discussions, look at what both sides want to achieve and look at what both sides have to give. And then ask:

- What is an easy give for me, that is of high benefit to them?
- What is an easy give for them, that is of high benefit to me?

This is a key process to win-win negotiation. If you get skilled at spotting these, you will find the whole negotiation process pleasurable and you will be very successful in your career.

The 3 rules for concessions

The three rules for concessions are that they should be:

- logical
- linked to a concession in return, and
- labelled.

Make your concessions logical

Your whole negotiation should be logical, of course. Any position you hold, any request you make, should be able to be backed up with a logical argument. Remember your Maximum Plausible Position? That is, even your most extreme request needs to stay within the bounds of plausibility.

And then any concession from there needs to be justifiable, you need to explain why you are making this concession. Otherwise it will not be valued and, worse, you can lose credibility.

Giving them the Tuesday rate

Sometimes your reason is less plausible than others but you should always have a reason of some sort.

I once found myself negotiating with a certain client for a piece of work, and I went in at quite a high price. They called me to say

---

that they really wanted to work with me but they simply could not afford it so sadly it was no deal. Now I had to find a way to accept a lower price, whilst keeping face and appearing credible.

My reason was along the lines of "Well, I give discounts on Tuesdays so if we did the work on Tuesdays we could come to a deal". Not very plausible really! But it worked, they believed me and both sides were happy.

But do be careful: a completely nonsensical reason may end up in losing credibility. And if your counterparty comes up with a "Tuesday" reason for their concession, allow them to keep face.

Make your concessions linked to something in return

Always make sure you get something in return for your concession.

As we have seen, the principle of reciprocity means that in many cases your counterparty will respond with a concession quite naturally. And if you have a good working relationship with them and there is trust you will not have to specifically make a request.

However, you may have to nudge their elbow and ask for something. If you do this, again make your request and the link to your own concession very logical. For example, you can suggest that you would be able to give them the discounted price if they bought a larger volume upfront because the set-up costs would be relatively lower.

Exploring possible concessions

It may not always be obvious what the return concession would be or, indeed, what your concession might be in return for a move they make.

In these cases, use that great phrase "What if...?".

"What if we were to pay your asking price, what could you include that would make it worth our while?"

Or "What if you were to drop that clause from the contract, what could we do that would still address your needs there?"

Here you are inviting them to explore with you the best trade you can make together. The advantage of using conditional language like this is that there is no commitment involved. They will respond with a suggestion and you still have the chance to agree to it or not. This frees up the discussion to explore possibilities that may not lead to anything but they increase your chances of finding a breakthrough.

Haggling on price

If there is only one variable involved in the negotiation (actually, very rarely the case), for example you are haggling in a market on the price of a vase, the psychology of bargaining expects concessions as we have seen.

Furthermore, depending on your market, it expects more than one. Rather than drop from £30 to £20 in one go, suggest £25, then £22, then £20. The other party will feel they have done better, even if £20 is what you intended to pay all along.

And making smaller and smaller concessions gives the illusion that you are reaching your bottom-line, the point beyond which you will not go.

Splitting the difference

Splitting the difference is a common form of mutual concession. It is not necessarily a rational solution but it may break through an impasse.

One tactic used is where your counterparty happily agrees to splitting the difference then reports at the next meeting that their boss would not accept it and they need a further compromise. If they do this, again get something else in return or call their bluff.

It is better to let them suggest splitting the difference because then they will own it more and they are less likely to renege in such circumstances.

Label your concessions

The third rule of concessions is that you label them. Do not rely on your counterparty to notice them and appreciate the effort you are making. Instead, make it very clear to them.

Spell out:

- the concession you are making and the reasoning behind it
- the cost of this for you
- the benefit for them.

Spend time explaining your position and legitimising it, do not budge too easily. For the concession to count, they need to notice and acknowledge it.

If you get to a point that you cannot go beyond, again explain why. It is more likely to be respected if there is a reason.

Responding to an extreme opening offer

The Strong Win-Win approach says start by finding out the interests of all parties. The old-school approach says start by finding the opening *positions* of all sides and from there haggle your way to a price somewhere in the middle. The positional approach has a dilemma: do you start with your opening figure or by asking theirs?

Thomas Edison benefitted by keeping quiet until the other party revealed their position, a position much better than he had hoped. His first invention was a stock-ticker which he sold to the Gold & Stock Telegraph Company in 1869. This was an economic boom time, after the end of the Civil War had led to a massive investment in railways and the telegraph industry, opening up the continent and allowing the economy to flourish. He had hoped for $5,000 but was prepared to accept $3,000. Fortunately, he let his machine do the talking for him because the Gold & Stock Telegraph Company were so impressed by it and how much money it would make them, they offered him $40,000.

However, sometimes there is a benefit by mentioning the first figure because, in doing so, you set the anchor. Anchoring is a psychological process by which we come to a 'fair' value for something and, specifically, it is when a figure is mentioned, the final fair value arrived at is likely to be affected by that figure.

It is why people selling a property have an advantage over those buying because they set a price at which the property is advertised. This figure now becomes an anchor and is likely to impact where the deal is finally made. Similarly, it is why estate agents will show you a property outside of your budget because when they then show you properties within your budget, but at the top end of the range, you will think them comparatively cheap (the easy way to counter this, by the way, is give the agent a lower figure to start off with).

So the positional approach has this dilemma, Strong Win-Win cuts through it by starting with interests. But what if they start the proceedings and open with an offer? As we saw at the beginning of the chapter, the best thing is to ignore it and enquire to the reasons behind it.

But what if their opening is quite an extreme offer? You will need to make sure you are not affected by the anchor.

You can do this by changing the units of measurement! Then go through your own valuation process (based on different methods and assumptions to theirs), put in your own figures (aggressive or stretch) and come to your own figure, which will be lower and will be the new anchor. What is more, it will not be measured relative to their opening offer and so will diminish their anchoring effect even further.

Typically, in a haggle, the final agreed price ends up half-way between the two opening offers. So if this really is a one-variable deal, make your counter offer such that the mid-point ends up at your target price. If they have made an extreme offer, this means you will have to make one too and you will have to be able to justify it but equally justify why you are open to negotiation.

Putting things in their best light

There is an internet email hoax that has been doing the rounds for several years in various guises. It describes how a professional genealogist had been researching her own background and came across an ancestor who had been a horse thief in the wild west and was hung for his crimes.

On further investigation, she finds that she shares this ancestor with a senior politician (it has been Hilary Clinton, Al Gore,

---

George Bush and others in different versions) . She writes to this politician to inform them of her findings and receives the reply that this common ancestor had "passed away during an important civic function held in his honour when the platform on which he was standing had collapsed".

Similar amusing stories exist about ancestors who occupied the Chair of Applied Electricity at an august public institution – meaning he suffered the death penalty by electrocution!

How you say things can make a big difference.

Saying things without actually saying things

In negotiation talks it is very helpful if you can say something...without actually saying it.

There are a few reasons for this. The first is that sometimes you might like to explore a subject, not knowing whether it will lead to a solution or not. In such a case, you do not want to commit to anything until it has been fully discussed; you do not want to be held to ransom for saying something that you did not really mean.

The second reason is around keeping face. By implying something, without actually saying it explicitly, it can allow either party to agree to something without losing face.

And the third is around ownership of the idea. They are much more likely to agree to your idea if you let them come up with it. People like to own ideas: if you tell someone to do something, they will probably resist; if you make a suggestion, you have a 50-50 chance they will go along with it; if you let them come up with your idea, they will be passionate about it.

Signalling without saying

Signalling is another way to save face; it allows you to shift your position in such a way that it does not look like you are shifting or, on the other hand, allow the other party to budge in such a way that it does not look like they are doing so.

A signal is an indication that the negotiator is prepared to move if the other party is prepared to move too, but it is a coded indication. It can sound very strong and robust but implicit within it will be a pointer to an opening for the possibility of negotiation.

Consider: "I can only say a very firm 'no' as things stand". This seems unequivocal and you can even bang the table as you say it. However, hidden away in the phrase 'as things stand' is a signal that there may be room for manoeuvre. As things stand: firm no; if things were to change (and I leave that up to you to decide how they change): maybe yes.

Or consider the difference between "It would be impossible to meet that deadline" and "It would be very difficult to meet that deadline". They are almost identical and can be said equally stridently. However, the second one allows for movement in a way that the first does not.

In both of these examples, you can indicate flexibility without losing face.

Saving face

To save face, a concession can be hidden using vague wording or hiding it in a side letter or appendix. It is still part of the agreement, but it is obscured by being placed in Appendix 23B.

In the Northern Ireland peace process, the British government did not want to negotiate with Sinn Fein unless the IRA had already decommissioned their weapons. The IRA, however, would not do that because they did not trust the British government. A possible solution was parallel decommissioning – starting the process of verifiable decommissioning as the talks began.

An independent body was set up to recommend how to solve this and other problems. Prior to releasing their recommendations, as part of the sounding process, they met with John Major, the British Prime Minister and told him they

---

would be recommending parallel decommissioning. Major said the British government would have to reject it and this would be politically troublesome.

Later, in a private meeting, a government aide (on instructions, clearly) asked if the body had considered making it as a suggestion *in a separate body to the main text*. Not being a part of the main body of recommendations meant that the recommendation could still be made but in such a way that the government had more political leeway to accept its core message.

Face-saving happens in many ways. When Iran and the U.S. negotiated their settlement of the hostage crisis in 1980-81, the agreement was mediated through Algeria. To enable the deal, the final wording suggested any Iranian concessions were made to Algeria and not to America.

And when the Soviet Union negotiated their pulling out from Afghanistan there was no mention of the removal of their troops at all! Instead, it mentioned more generally the withdrawal of "foreign" troops. (Is that "foreign" as in Soviet, Mr Gorbachev?)

Let them come up with your ideas

Another simple way to say something without actually saying it is to tell a story about it. Tell them of a similar situation to the one you are facing and the resolution (which is, of course, favourable from your perspective) that was arrived at and then let them come to the conclusion that it would work for them too. Do not suggest it as a solution, you may even actively indicate why that other situation is different to the current circumstances, but let them come to their own conclusions.

The example can be a current story in the newspapers or a story about a well-known company or individual.

- "Did you see in the news, Branson's in a similar situation. What he's doing is..."

- "I'm not suggesting we do this ourselves, but what some companies do in this situation is..."

Or it could be personal:

- "A colleague of mine had a similar situation and what they did was to...I'm not saying we do that here but...",
- "I had a similar situation with a previous client and what they found useful was..."

Tell the story, say you are not suggesting we use it here then let them think about it and a day later they will probably come up with it as a solution.

Alternatively, come up with their ideas

Ownership of ideas is very powerful. If it is your idea, they may support it. If it is their idea, they will fight for it.

So use this. If you do have a good idea, let it come across as theirs. If it was their idea, acknowledge it as such. If it was part of a joint discussion, link it to something they, in particular, said. Use phrases like "building on your idea..." or "your idea has triggered a thought...".

You can do this even if it is completely opposite to their suggestion but be careful, it can come across as disingenuous.

 Action points

Concessions are an important aspect of bargaining.

▸ Start by trading items low cost for you and high value for them in return for those that are high value for you and low cost to them

▸ All concessions should be logical, labelled and linked to a concession in return

▸ Use the magic words, "What if...?"; they enable you to say things without being committed to them

▸ Put your message in its best light but be aware they may do the same, so dig behind their words with probing questions

▸ Allow them ownership of the good ideas.

8.5 DEALING WITH DIRTY TRICKS

Now it has been known, in the history of negotiation, for an unscrupulous party to play some devious trick in order to optimise their gain from the deal. In some cultures (geographical or industry), this is standard. Indeed, such tricks are *taught* in some old-school books and courses.

We hope that if you have followed everything written to date, this will not occur in your negotiation because the other party love you so much they would not dream of such a thing. However, it happens. So it would be remiss not to dedicate a few pages to listing some of the tricks people play and how to manage them. Strong Win-Win means confidence to play win-win because you know you can recognise and respond to anything underhand.

Of course, some of you might read a section entitled "Dirty Tricks" and respond, "At last, this is what I've been looking for!" and you will read this next section as a "How to..." manual.

Don't even think about it. Any such ploy will go lose-lose as soon as it is found out. We saw in the studies of the Ultimatum Game, that if the other party thinks they have been scammed, they will sabotage the whole deal, even if it hurts themselves in doing so. And if they have no recourse in the deal itself, they can always find out where you live!

Even if they never find out for certain, there will be suspicions. You will lose trust and all its accompanying dividends. They will be guarded, they will be defensive, they will not fully commit to any deal. You will only get half a deal.

What makes a dirty trick dirty?

The problem with dirty tricks is the difficulty in telling whether they are dirty or not. One thing is for sure: they will not signal it for you. Do not expect them to laugh evilly "mwah-hah-hah-hah!" as they do it. Instead, they will be smiling, shaking your hand and saying "Let's do lunch soon. You'll have to tell me about that charity of yours, it sounds such a great cause, I'd love to help out".

What, in one circumstance, is a perfectly valid tactic can, in another, be a dirty trick. Many of the behaviours espoused in this book can, in the wrong hands, be a sneaky ploy. Many of the behaviours in this book can be used equally by psychopaths or psaints.

If they ring last minute with a hitch, for example, how do we know if it is real or a tactic? If their team are all for the deal except for one person, who needs more convincing – are they playing good cop-bad cop or is it genuine?

Muddying the waters further, it is rarely a black-or-white issue: dirty can involve shades of grey. If I use certain words and you take a certain inference from them, is the cause of misunderstanding with me or with you? If I allow you to take a certain inference, even though I know it is incorrect, am I being fair, mischievous or downright wrong? Presenting your case in its best light is a perfectly fair behaviour in negotiation. Indeed, barristers are professionally bound to represent their client optimally, which may mean presenting some facts and not others, it may mean using certain words and not others.

Most people would say it is wrong to break the law in order to get a better deal. Many would say it is wrong to lie too but there are an equal number who accept that lying is part of the business world. And have you ever said something like, 'The lowest I can go is £1,000' when you know actually you would probably accept £750. Well, this is a lie. And yet the majority of people would feel ok saying it in a negotiation.

We get into very murky waters. Who really has never been guilty of such fibs? Indeed, many would urge it as negotiation best practice.

Trickster beware!

The problem is that all this greyness impacts the trickster too. If your deviousness raises suspicions, it will significantly reduce the level of trust. They might not be able to put their finger on exactly what it is, but they just sense something is not quite kosher.

They may well retaliate, they may pull out altogether, they will certainly be extra cautious in any further dealings with you. There will be, at the very least, a distrust tax to pay.

Fair play if your deed was dastardly, you were caught red-handed and cannot complain. But what if you were bending the truth *just a little*? The other person does not know this and their reaction may be out of proportion to the deed. Tough, you brought it on yourself.

So, when you tell a little white lie or pull a harmless trick, be careful. It may back-fire.

Ruse or fact – how to tell

In many instances, there is a simple way to tell whether it is legitimate or a sneaky ploy. It is to accept the problem at face value and work with the other party to find a solution. If genuine, they will be happy to do so; if not, they will find excuses why it is not possible.

Deadlines, for example, can be used to create pressure to force concessions. Research has shown that negotiators tend to make lower demands, increase concessions and lower their expectations under pressure of time because of the belief that if it goes past the deadline circumstances will change so that it is either not possible at all or it is at considerably worse terms. Unscrupulous negotiators create false deadlines to exploit this.

But deadlines can sometimes be moved or partially met ("Ok, we need the client-facing material by the deadline but the project support material is not so urgent and can be delivered later"). Or perhaps you can agree to the deadline but only if certain conditions of yours are met ("To deliver it so quickly we will have to put extra resources on it so it will cost more"). If your counterparty is genuine, they will be happy to find a solution that suits everyone.

Another example is when your counterparty says they are not authorised to sign the deal and, after reaching agreement, they take it to their boss who has the final say – perfectly legitimate or a sneaky manoeuvre. If the latter, the boss does not sign off without further concessions on your part.

This is frequently a genuine question of authority and not a trick. You have agreed a great deal, now the challenge is to go back to your respective bosses and sell it to them. They have not built up any of the rapport or understandings of the full complications of the decisions that led to the final agreement. Hence, they may require persuading.

So, work with your counterparty to solve the problem. Discuss the bosses' criteria and requirements from the deal and work together to help each other sell it in. Ask what each decision-maker is looking for and what they will need to say yes.

If you do suspect a ploy, though, let them run it past their boss (or their mum or whoever) but stress that everything is agreed contingent on the whole package being agreed. If any further changes are required, they will need reviewing in the light of the whole deal.

How to lose an airline

In November, 1999, Richard Branson announced the launch of Virgin Blue, a new budget airline to operate in Australia, New Zealand and the South Pacific. It involved an initial investment of A$10m. A year later, its success brought an offer from the CEO of Singapore Airlines of A$250m. A twenty five times return on investment within a year! Surely, an offer Branson could not refuse.

The only strange thing about the offer was that it was in the form of an ultimatum. They had to agree within 24 hours or the deal would be off and Singapore Airlines would instead commit to a massive investment programme in Ansett, their subsidiary, a major competitor to Virgin Blue.

Branson mulled the offer with Brett Godfrey, his Chief Executive. Although it was difficult to refuse the offer, they agreed there was something fishy about the ultimatum. They decided to turn it down; turn down a profit of A$240m from a year's work!

The next day, it was announced that Ansett was to fold. It had been a bluff, after all. There *had* been something fishy. Ansett were in no fit state to compete with Virgin Blue and it was the ultimatum that flagged this up to Branson and Godfrey.

Singapore Airlines came out with absolutely nothing from this. They lost a whole airline and had nothing to show for it. If instead, they had sat down with Branson and suggested a co-operative venture, combining the best of Virgin Blue with the best of Ansett, they would probably have got a deal, after all, they were already partners in a different venture.

Given the state of Ansett it may not have been much of a deal. But wait till you hear the coda. Eighteen months later, Virgin Blue was listed on the Australian Stock Exchange, raising A$2.3bn! Any deal Singapore swung to land part of a A$2.3bn business would have been preferable to where they ended up.

How to protect yourself against them

Needless to say, prophylactic measures are recommended over therapeutic – make sure the situation never arises in the first place. And the best way to inoculate yourself is to use the Strong Win-Win system.

So, firstly, prepare: know your stuff, know their world better than they do. Then they will recognise that they will not be able to get away with any ploys, that it will instantly be detected, so they will not try.

Secondly, related, is show your credibility. The stronger you come across, the less likely they are to try anything on. Think about it: no one would try to pull a fast one on Mike Tyson, would they? And, at the same time, focus on building a strong relationship. People do not cheat people they like. People do not cheat others who are "one of us".

And be alert. If they give you a product on a free trial period, be aware that it will be harder to negotiate terms and conditions when the trial period ends because you have got used to having it. (This is known as "the puppy dog ploy" – if someone gives you a puppy dog on a free trial period, you are never going to give it back, are you?!)

Or if they impress you with big promises and big figures, be alert to this. Stay with the facts on the ground, do not let yourself be seduced.

Or if they bring their in-house contract as the draft for the discussions, be alert they are now playing on "home ground" and have an advantage. They will be comfortable, knowing their way around it and you may not have the opportunity to read it through and digest it as much as you would like, so they may be able to sneak things through that are not obvious but have critical impact on its implementation. And thirdly, any red ink that you insist on will be viewed as a concession. They will end up giving away much less than if you had both drawn up the contract together, starting from a blank page.

At the other end of the negotiation, it is not unheard of for them to fax you over a copy of the contract to be signed, having slipped in new clauses or undiscussed changes, hoping you do not notice and, in happy ignorance, sign away. There are unscrupulous people out there, some of them are dressed very well and smile a lot. Read your contract.

How to respond

But sometimes our inoculations are not enough and we still meet behaviour we find unhelpful. On such occasions, your behaviour should lean more on the strength side of Strong Win-Win, whilst still maintaining rapport.

So manage your response, do not let yourself be outraged, tempting though it is. By staying calm you will be able to make a reliable decision on the best way forward. Maybe, if it really is not that important, you can let it pass and play along with it. You may even be able to turn it to your advantage.

Alternatively, ask questions to clarify exactly what they mean and their reasons. As with dealing with difficult people, step into their shoes and see it from their point of view. This will give you a lot of understanding about their motives and this, in turn, will inform your best strategy to combat it.

You do not have to buy into their reality. If they have given you a deadline, you can always call their bluff and let the deadline pass. If they give you a take-it-or-leave-it offer, you can still make further offers in response. In fact, you can make several, with conditions to each, and you are effectively continuing the negotiation even without their input. Or if they are trying to scare you by talking about the competition, remember – there is a reason why they are talking to you. Re-focus on that reason and you strengthen your hand.

As ever, remind them of their bigger picture goals and their Plan B and let them know of your Plan B. And remind them of the benefits of collaborating towards a mutually beneficial win-win solution. This should re-focus them on behaving in a more principled way so, again, give them a way out that enables them to save face.

If they still do not recant, this will be a time for the verify part of trust but verify! Again, if you can do this in a diplomatic way to allow them a way out, that will be better. But if they are not helping themselves, call their bluff in whatever way is required.

The Strong Win-Win method believes in helping people towards collaboration, to a degree taking responsibility for their collaboration. And part of this is, as they do not respond to the carrot, slowly warn of and then introduce the stick. So call them on their behaviour, again tactfully if you can but if that does not work, directly. And let them know you operate by the rules of Tit-For-Tat so if they want the best deal on the table, they have to negotiate in good faith.

And, as a last resort, consider your Plan B – do you really want to stay in the deal? If not, leave, but if so, consider what power options you have for enforcing an honest modus operandi.

CHAPTER 9: TRUST BUT VERIFY

9.1 SEEK TO TRUST

So you find yourself in a negotiation and the guy on the other side of the table has horns, cloven feet and a tail and there is a slight whiff of brimstone in the air. You say "So that's agreed, then?" and he replies "Certainly, it's a pleasure doing business with you" and bursts into an evil cackle. With your hand shielding your mouth, you lean over to your colleague and whisper, "There's something about him that I don't fully trust".

When it comes to win-win, trust is a key question.

And some people are harder to trust than others. Michael Milken was famously dubbed the Junk Bond King and was the most successful financier on Wall Street in the 1980's. In 1986, Fred Joseph, the Chief Executive of Drexel, Milken's employer, gave the company's bonus pool to Milken to divide out as he saw fit.

Milken distributed $150m to his colleagues, including $10m to Jim Dahl, his top salesperson. He told Dahl, "I really can't pay you any more or you'd be making more than me." Strangely, Milken's maths must have somehow contained an error – he actually awarded himself a bonus of $550m. This was more than the entire profit of the company!

In 1989 he was indicted on 98 counts of racketeering and fraud. He was sentenced to 10 years in prison but released after less than two.

Milken is just one of a long list of high-profile fraudsters, standing alongside the likes of Ivan Boesky, Bernie Madoff, Kenneth Lay, Jeffrey Skilling and Bernie Ebbers in the roll-call of shame. But these are the ones who were caught. And these are the ones we know about. What about our guy, the man across the table? Smiling, shaking our hands, saying "Pleasure doing business with you" – will we one day see his mug-shot splashed across the newspapers?

Our strategy to date has been to avoid the quite ridiculous inefficiencies of the arm-wrestle and instead play the arm-game. And we do this in real-life by ensuring the other party also wants to play win-win and then by working together, on a problem-solving basis, to create greater value that is shared for all to benefit. And we have seen many strategies that will bring them around to win-win thinking and many ways to make sure the problem is solved.

But there is a big assumption involved here – namely, that we can trust our counterparty.

What if they have not actually come around to our way of win-win thinking, despite what they tell us? How can we tell? What if we think we can trust them for now but they could renege at the slightest opportunity? What if we are quite sure they are totally evil but we still need to do a deal?

In Chapter 7, we saw how to increase someone's trustableness. Here we will look at the situation where trust is not enough. "Trust in me," sang Kaa, the python in Walt Disney's "The Jungle Book, as he slowly wrapped his coils around Mowgli. It is not enough to trust someone just because they say so, we cannot afford to be naive.

We need to be clever about it and the Strong Win-Win approach has a strategy which can be summed up in the phrase "Trust but verify" and is built on four pillars:

- Seek to trust. Trust is a good thing, there is a return on it.
- But know how to tell if you can trust someone
- Know what to do to increase their trustworthiness
- Know what to do if you really cannot trust them at all.

In Russian, trust but verify translates as "Doveryai, no proveryai" and it became the by-word of Reagan and Gorbachev as they talked their way through the history-making nuclear disarmament negotiations between America and the Soviet Union. Two leaders, with no reason for trusting their counterparty but every incentive for doing so, used it as their touchstone as they negotiated the end to the Cold War.

Trust but verify. Absolutely trust. And absolutely verify. And we will see exactly how to do this in practice.

Trust is good

A 2002 study by Watson Wyatt found that high-trust organisations are likely to produce three times as much shareholder value than low-trust organisations.

We can give some examples. Huntsman Chemical sold a share in their company to Great Lakes Chemicals at an agreed price of $54m. In the six months that it took before Great Lakes finally

---

completed the processing of the deal, the value of that share had risen to $250m. Great Lakes suggested re-negotiating the price to $150m, effectively splitting the windfall. Huntsman refused the extra $100m and stuck to their originally agreed $54m.

If you think Huntsman Chemicals were naive in doing this, they are a company valued at $8bn. Their methods have served them well.

Not big enough for you? Ok, how about Johnson and Johnson? Jim Burke, their CEO, says "I have found that by trusting people until they prove themselves unworthy of that trust, a lot more happens."

Or Warren Buffett who bought McLane Distribution, a $23bn company, from Walmart. He said, "We did no 'due diligence'. We knew everything would be exactly as Walmart said it would be, and it was." As a result, the deal was struck in a one hour meeting and completed within a month.

The no-trust tax and how to avoid it

When you do not trust, there is a tax to pay.

Think about it, if you bought a house from your dad and he said, 'Look, I've been living here for 20 years and I can tell you there is no structural problem with it', you would believe him, and you would save yourself £1000 for an extensive structural survey. When you buy from a stranger, there is not the same degree of trust so you pay up. This is a tax that is payable when trust is not there.

Now, as with all taxes, sometimes it is worth paying. But overall, it is a brake on proceedings and the greater trust we can work with, the more efficiently things will go.

How slow would things be if you had to run chemical tests on every pint of milk you buy from the supermarket to make sure it was safe? Every second of the day we place huge amounts of trust in the world around us and at any point that we do not trust, it slows us down enormously.

Life is quicker and cheaper when we trust.

Johnson and Johnson and Huntsman Chemicals are hugely successful companies built on trust. Warren Buffett saved himself time and money by trusting. These industry leaders see the dividend that is collected from trust.

Can we ever fully trust?

We can never fully trust. The other person may be lying, they may have a personality disorder or they may be spawn of the devil. What is worse, it is not always obvious when we can and when we cannot, you cannot always smell brimstone.

In fact, even if we can trust the person in front of us, even if they are the coital fruits of the Dalai Lama and Mother Teresa themselves, there may be forces beyond their control that mean they cannot deliver as promised.

But babies and bath-water spring to mind here. Just because we cannot trust completely does not mean we should stop trusting altogether. There may be a chance a meteorite will hit my apartment today but that does not mean I should wear a crash helmet in my kitchen.

Trust is cultural

Of course, there are cultural aspects to it. If you are in a war-zone, you may be safer trusting less. On the other hand, if you find yourself in a convent for the Sisters of Our Lady of Mercy, you could probably afford to trust a little more. (Unless you are playing poker for money, then I would watch them like a hawk! Well, that is my experience anyway...)

By culture, we can mean geographically or racially defined culture and levels of trust can vary significantly at this level. Francis Fukuyama wrote an excellent book called "Trust. The Social Virtues and the Creation of Prosperity" in which he tracks the relationship between trust in a society and its level of wealth.

Alternatively, we can mean industry defined culture, like the bond traders described by Michael Lewis, where they actively looked for the fool to exploit.

Indeed, in some cultures it is very much their job *not* to trust. If you are in risk management or insurance, for example, it is your job to assume the worst. In aspects of law, medicine, policing and other such areas, it is also your job to assume the worst. So if you are negotiating with someone from these fields, do not necessarily expect them to trust you.

In some cultures it can be safe, in others you will be the fool to trust. If you want to know how much you can trust, know your culture.

Trust is contextual

Trust is contextual too and we saw in Chapter 7 that, therefore, we can sometimes manage the context to increase the individual's level of honesty. Even if this is not possible, we can still examine the circumstances for further clues as to whether we can trust them or not.

Engel's meta-study of the Dictator Game experiments and other studies have found people are more trustworthy if:

-        they are elderly (in fact, in the Dictator Game study there was a very strong correlation with age all the way up from children, through students, through middle-age, to pensioner. Maybe the octogenarian Rupert Murdoch will finally become more generous in his dotage...yeah, right!)

- they are female
- *you* are female (people are more honest with women, perhaps given the previous finding, because they can expect honesty in return)
- they deal with you face to face
- they believe you are deserving (for example, you are a not-for-profit organisation)
- the more win-win it is (that is, the greater the extra value created).

Similarly, the studies found that they are less trustworthy if:

- they can conceal their dishonesty (that is, they think they will not be caught)
- they have to work hard to achieve that which is to be shared
- there are other people around also talking tough
- they make their decision in a group
- they are asked to be benevolent repeatedly

- they think you are doing ok for yourself as it is.

Therefore, seek to trust, you will be paid a handsome dividend. But investments are not guaranteed and so it is with trust. And just as there are tools to assess the wisdom of an investment, so there are techniques to gauge whether the person in front of you is reliable and we will look at these now.

9.2 HOW TO TELL IF YOU CAN TRUST THEM

Can they deliver?

In God, we trust. Everyone else, we run the normal verification procedures. The first concerns their capability to deliver or not. The second is regards to their intention. Can they? Will they?

Capability is easier to assess than intention so let us address this first. You need to:

- Check their track record
- Check their skills
- Check their knowledge.

The simplest way is to find out if they have done this before. You will be able to get some idea in conversation but remember: trust but verify. Do your research, talk to others who have conducted business with them. Happily, these factors are relatively 'concrete' and so can be checked quite easily.

There is still the question that they may not deliver due to matters beyond their control. This is more a case of trust in the circumstances as opposed to trust in the person. To gauge this the first thing to do is verify their power to deliver. Then ask:

- What might prevent them delivering?
- What is the likelihood of that (those) arising?
- What are the early warning signals?
- What alternative plans would be necessary in the instance they do arise?

Then keep checking in.

Will they deliver?

"Can they deliver?" is the easy question, "*Will* they deliver?" is less tangible and so harder to assess.

This is a question of trusting their personal integrity and, unfortunately, there are no easy guidelines. There is no Pinocchio-style giveaway, they do not wear a liar's hat.

So, much as you may hope for a cute little lie-detecting technique here, a magic question and a sure-fire facial tic, I am afraid nothing in the current science of deception suggests such a thing exists.

Simon Horton

Nothing beats doing your research and checking the facts. Try to get hold of as many sources of information on the matter as you can and get other opinions and perspectives.

What is their track record, have they generally been truthful or not? Have their facts and assertions been reliable or not? Remember, there can be shades of grey – are there some areas where they are reliable and others not? Talk to others who have worked with them and find out their experience.

Are they happy to push back on something that is not realistic? Have they ever gone the extra mile and over-delivered. If something has gone wrong, have they taken accountability? All of these are signs of integrity and greater trustworthiness.

Have they made a credible commitment already? Have they made a *public* commitment? Are they investing in it: financial, time, reputation or other resources? Have they done anything concrete towards making it happen? The more they have committed already, the more confident you can be they will see it through. If they have burnt their bridges, there is no going back so this would be a sure sign you can trust them.

Trust but verify. Do whatever research is required. Ask to see the evidence, the basis of their calculations, ask other people, do the research. You can easily do this without threatening their personal trustworthiness. You can say your boss has asked to see the figures or it is in case they are moved on to a different project and you have to deal with someone new. Or start with the emphasis on your commitment to the verification process – "Obviously you will want quarterly reports from us to show you what we are doing and we would expect the same from you."

Check the direct facts but also look for other indirect clues. Is it consistent with other facts? Ask what other behaviour or facts would be consistent with telling the truth or telling a lie? Is the story plausible? Is it internally consistent? Which is the simplest explanation – that they are lying or they are telling the truth?

When King Solomon was faced with two women claiming motherhood of a baby, he proposed cutting it in half and dividing it between them. The first 'mother' agreed – uh-uh! This is unlikely to be the response of a mother. The second refused and would rather give the baby away than see it cut in half. Their responses showed who was telling the truth.

Can you think of such a test that would indicate truth or non-truth? Or predict some other early warning indicator? Test them with something you know the answer to or test them with something where you know they may have a temptation to lie.

For example, deliberately fail to notice something to your benefit and see if they point it out. Or ask them to do a task that requires effort on their part, if they deliver then they are probably serious about the deal. If they return with a reason why they cannot produce, there is a higher chance they will not go ahead with the deal, despite any fine words on their part.

A very simple test of their integrity: drop your pen. If they pick it up for you, you are in safe hands. There are two types of people in the world – those who will pick it up for you, those who will not. The former are the carers, they will look out for you. The latter, of course, are not necessarily evil but they do think more of themselves. Or, of course, they have a bad back.

Detecting Deceit

Detecting deceit is not easy. Beware, there are some very good liars out there! Some people are almost impossible to catch out, especially if they have convinced themselves of their truth. There are groups of people for whom it is almost their job to lie. Politicians, head-hunters ringing up for information ("I'm doing a market survey..."). They do it every day, it is expected of them, do not believe them! Is the person you are dealing with one of these? Check the culture.

Paul Ekman is considered a leader in the field of lie-detection. Amongst many more professionally reputable claims, he is the principal consultant to the television series, "Lie To Me". He has studied over 20,000 people and found that the large majority of people have *only a 50% success rate* at detecting truth or lie. In other words, they could just as well have flipped a coin. This was true even amongst professionals – judges, FBI, police, barristers, polygraphers, forensic psychiatrists and similar professions.

However, he has found a very small number of people, whom he calls Truth Wizards, who consistently get a success rate of 80% or higher. Only 50 people out of the 20,000 studied achieve this rate.

To detect deceit, he suggests:

1)   looking for contradictions in their account.
2)   looking for hesitation (to imply thinking about it)
3)   looking for vagueness of details

4)   or for too many details (it will have obviously have been planned and rehearsed)

5)   alluding or asking about the emotion of what is concealed, it is much harder to conceal the emotion

6)   checking the genuineness of any emotion in the facial expression. We often fake a smile, or fake enthusiasm, but it is possible to see whether it is genuine or not.

Of course, any individual signal may not indicate deception at all. A hand to the mouth may indicate garlic at lunchtime and shifting around on the chair may indicate too tight underwear. That is all.

A truth-teller is likely to give away many of these signs anyway if they think they are not believed. Similarly in a high-stakes situation, they may be nervous anyway and display some of these signals despite telling the truth.

Oh, where is that magic question?! Where is that sure-fire facial tic?! I am afraid none of these questions will give an unfailing answer: press button, click, whirr, and the lie-o-meter says...trust! If only it were so easy.

Instead, Ekman and others suggest:

1)   Looking for clusters of indications, especially in different channels, rather than working from any single one.

2)   Looking for *changes* in behaviour. Lack of eye contact means nothing if that is their normal way but if they normally give a lot of eye contact then suddenly look away when a particular issue is raised, this is more significant.

3)   Looking for patterns. If there is a change in behaviour with a particular topic, move away from the topic and look to see if they revert to their norm. Then bring it up again and look to see if the atypical behaviour recurs. Test and re-test.

4)   If you suspect something because you have counter-evidence, hold it back, do not present it till later, it will give them a chance to develop a story that is inconsistent with the evidence.

5)   And be wary of the confirmation bias. If you have a suspicion that the other person is not telling the truth, you may look for (and therefore find) evidence for this and ignore any counter-evidence. It is important to remain objective and open to proof and counter-proof.

One more caveat: much of the above findings derive from research on suspects in a crime interview situation. Your negotiation may not be conducted in such a manner! You will have to be more subtle in your supposings.

Using body language to detect skilled deceivers

Body language is often thought of as one of the keys to telling if someone is lying. And it is true, just think of the good old blush – it is an unconscious expression of a feeling or thought process that takes place way below the levels of our control. It can be very hard to prevent and so it can communicate our thoughts, despite our attempts to conceal them.

Joe Navarro spent 25 years as an FBI agent and was one of the original founding members of their elite Behavioural Analysis Programme. He has written extensively on body language, not least for poker players, along with Phil Hellmuth, the nine times World Series of Poker Champion.

He encourages you to observe their non-verbal response when you:

- Talk about specific parts of the deal or clauses in the contract
- Ask questions about a certain area (it can tell you that there is something in that area they are not comfortable with, something you may not have been aware of before)
- Talk about delivery
- Ask them about possible problematic scenarios.

He echoes much of the other researchers in saying it is important to baseline the individual before jumping to any conclusions and look for variance from this baseline. Look for spikes around certain topics; move away from the topic and get them relaxed again, then bring it up again and see if the behaviour recurs. Even then there may be more than one possible cause for the behaviour, so you need to isolate the real cause.

If you think you are talking to a skilled deceiver, Navarro says not to focus on the face – the accomplished liar can control this. Instead, he emphasises the limbic system which is wired so deeply into our evolutionary programming that it is very hard to control.

In particular, look out for any behaviour that might be considered a fight, flight or freeze response. The feet are an important part of this system and, he says, often give away what the face is concealing. So look for feet pointing towards the exit, or energetic feet, bouncing up and down.

Other behaviours to look out for are known as pacifiers. These take place after an uncomfortable thought and they tend to be protective or soothing tactile gestures. Again, even the skilled deceiver is not always aware they are doing these.

Do they fancy you?

Barbara and Allen Pease also write on the topic of body language and would echo all that is written above. They also give advice on how to tell if someone fancies you!

Hey, it could be important in the negotiation, remember what we said about rapport?! (Ok, it's a shamelessly irrelevant aside but it is fun. And maybe it is not so irrelevant – we will see.)

Here is a list for some indicators of them fancying you. They:

- lean in towards you or sit or stand closer than normal
- point their feet or legs or body towards you
- look at your body
- touch you or something of yours
- touch themselves
- mirror how you sit or stand
- lick their lips.

If a woman fancies you, she will:

- make the face platter (hands underneath the chin, forming a presentation platform for the face)
- expose the neck or play with her hair
- cross/uncross her legs or play with her shoes
- preen herself or put on her lipstick
- sit up straight and put chest out
- tilt her hips or head to one side
- expose her wrists

- put handbag in close proximity or say "Look after my handbag, will you?" (handbags are *very* personal to a woman).

If a guy fancies you, he will:

- make himself look big by standing tall with his chest out and shoulders back
- possibly become more nervous around you
- be cheeky and try to make you laugh
- laugh at your jokes (he probably would not do otherwise!)
- remember what you say and refer back to it (again, sadly, he probably would not do otherwise!)

What has this to do with negotiation? Well, if you are looking for a new partner, that is one of the most important negotiations you will do in your life!

 Action points

Trust is the basis of successful negotiations that bring extra value to all parties involved. If there is one action points from this chapter it is to trust and build trust. But verify too:

▸ Look for verbal and non-verbal signals that may suggest discomfort or deceit

▸ Look for clusters and patterns and variations from their natural behaviour

▸ Most of all, check the facts first-hand.

9.3 INCREASE THEIR TRUSTWORTHINESS

We spent the whole of chapter 7 on increasing the other person's trustworthiness by moving them to a win-win mind-set at the beginning of the negotiation. In this section, we will look at what you can do as the deal is in progress, even as it closes, to maximise their dependability, although you are not 100% sure they are a win-win fanatic at all. And then, in the last section, we will look at what to do when you are 100% sure they are absolutely *not* converted to the win-win cause but you still have to do a deal.

Closing the deal correctly

Trust but verify. Absolutely trust. And absolutely verify. It is exactly this verification that enables you to trust. So make sure, as you close the deal, that verification procedures are put in place. Indeed, make sure that the other party is locked-in to its implementation then less verification will be necessary.

Some people view closing with a sense of mystery but if you set the negotiation up correctly, that is you go through all the steps we have mentioned to date, the deal should close itself. It is usually a very natural process. And if the deal is closed correctly, you will sleep soundly, confident it will be implemented the way you would like.

Flush out the "no"s!

Clearly, better written advice than spoken but before anything is signed, flush out the "no"s. (If your counterparty reaches for their handkerchief, they probably misheard their negotiation tutor).

By flushing out the "no"s, we mean remove any disagreements or potential obstacles to implementation (anything that may result in a "no") *before* the signature on the paper. Once it is written and signed, it is much harder to change.

In the beginning of a negotiation, vague language can serve a purpose. It enables the scope of the deal to be explored more loosely and for the dialogue to move in the right direction. Sticking blocks can be left unsettled as you progress on other aspects. However, as the deal approaches closure and the agreement is about to be put to paper, all potential disagreements need to be flushed out and resolved.

So many deals ultimately fail because of different interpretations. The two parties walk away with separate understandings of what was agreed and this inevitably causes trouble further down the line when the reality of the situation becomes exposed.

- "But you said..."
- "Yes, but what I was referring to was..."
- "Oh, I thought you meant..."

Unless it is nailed down tight at point of signature, there is a good chance they will weasel their way out when the opportunity arises. It is what people do. As Homer Simpson said, it is what separates us from the animals...except the weasel.

A great anti-weaselling device (AWD) which we have seen already is to get specific. If you are to put your signature to anything, make sure you know *exactly* what it means and what it entails. If you agree the project will be delivered by the end of the month – exactly what will get delivered? By whom? How will it be delivered? Does midnight, Sunday 31st count as the end of the month or does it need to be 5pm Friday 29th? Or before even?

We saw earlier how powerful the word "specifically" is, along with its buddies: precisely, particularly, exactly and so on. Use them. Make sure all potential disagreements are clarified. Pre-empt weaselling!

Be clear

United Nations Security Council Resolution 242 is one of the most cited documents in the Middle East conflict. It addresses the withdrawal of Israeli forces from land gained in the Six Day War in 1967.

There are two versions of the agreement. The first is in English and includes the call for the "Withdrawal of Israeli armed forces from territories occupied in the recent conflict". The second, with equal legal weight, is in French and has the corresponding line "Retrait des forces armées israéliennes des territoires occupés lors du récent conflit."

Despite agreement to its principles from all parties, years of hostilities have continued. Why? Because of one word, the simple

---

definite article ("the" in English, "des" in French) and how it is used in the two texts.

Withdrawal "*des* territoires occupés" means "withdrawal from the occupied territories" and therefore alludes to all territories occupied in the war. However, it could also mean withdrawal from just some of them. The English version, without the definite article, is even more equivocal.

This ambiguity was considered a diplomatic coup at the time because it allowed both parties to present their own version to their constituency.

Unfortunately, each party has since stuck to their interpretation and decades of war have followed as a result.

Don't sacrifice future peace for a temporary agreement.

Anticipate future scenarios

Potential for disagreement can hide in future scenarios. **To make the deal stick, anticipate possible events and the best responses to them.** It is much easier to agree these upfront than when they actually occur.

For example, what happens when one party wants to get out of the partnership? What happens if a particular external circumstance impacts the situation? What happens if a delivery does not meet the required standards and so on?

Identify the structural elements that may make this more likely and try to counter these in the agreement. And identify the knock-on effects of the agreement and how to take them into account in your agreed solution and the written agreement. Spend time with the other party thinking the deal through, how it is likely to progress, and what things may come up. It is better to pre-empt them now even if they are very low probability (but potentially high-impact).

Future pace the deal: talk it through, using the present tense, as it is likely to progress. Take them through their side of the bargain, their actions and yours, and talk them through the benefits they will achieve.

This leads their brain through the scenarios and so there will be less of a surprise when anything does come up. This is especially important if you think there are likely to be tricky issues or the other party has a track record of not delivering.

Include post-agreement procedures

Despite the best of plans, things can still go awry so it is good to pre-empt these whilst things are still all smiles and handshakes.

Define your verification procedures now to both parties' satisfaction and include a disputes procedure to deal with any difficulty arising. Needless to say, the lightest approach is often the most successful, so simply communicate with the other party before anything becomes a significant problem. But have escalation trigger points and more formal problem resolution processes, just in case. Third parties may play a part in both verification and dispute resolution.

Howard Raiffa, Professor of Management Economics at Harvard, suggests the concept of a post-settlement settlement. This means that after an agreement has been reached in a negotiation, it is put to a 3rd party who looks to see if they can improve it. Either side, of course, can veto any suggested modifications.

In fact, it does not need to be a 3rd party, it can be the same two parties. Part of their agreement process is to include reviews, looking for improvements to the deal. Again, either side can veto any changes and use the original agreement as the final one.

Get it in writing

Get it in writing. This is simple but fundamental.

Quite apart from protecting your posterior, written agreements involve a greater psychological commitment and are more likely to be delivered. This is true even when we negotiate with ourselves – we will be more successful in losing weight if we write down our goal and a target date. It is equally true in dealing with others.

Have the documents prepared already so they can be signed there and then. This reduces the chances of people changing their minds. If you prepare them, it enables you to define the terms of the agreement rather than the other side. Once given a contract, it is difficult to change a clause without it looking like further negotiation. Conversely, if they provide you with their template, you will be on the back foot if you request a lot of changes.

Having the documents prepared for the meeting also negates a particularly underhand practice whereby a party posts a copy of a contract, requesting signature, but said copy contains changes that were never agreed. If you do find yourself receiving a copy to sign by post or email, make sure it is identical to the one you agreed.

The downside of signing a document in the meeting, of course, is that it does not give you time to mull the full implications so if you feel you need this time, do take the agreement away with you to sign at your leisure.

How writing evolved

The very earliest writings developed precisely for establishing trust in negotiations and thereby enabling commercial transactions to take place more confidently.

As farming and trading of produce started to emerge in the Fertile Crescent over 10,000 years ago, small clay tokens would be used to represent different products and different amounts of each. To agree a transaction or record a loan, these tokens would be exchanged. For example, I may agree to fix the roof on your house and, in return, you would pay me 2 bushels of grain to be delivered at harvest time. As proof of this agreement, you would give me 2 tokens, each of which represented one bushel of grain.

The tokens were usually enclosed in an envelope made of soft clay and would press against it so you could see the contents without opening the envelope. As time went on, they realised the tokens were redundant, you could represent the produce traded simply by drawing the symbol on the envelope.

By the 3rd millennium BC, these symbols had developed into the cuneiform script of the Sumerian language and writing was born.

Go public

Go public with your agreement. For reasons of reputation, a public agreement is much more likely to be adhered to. Make sure that if they renege, the world (or specific individuals or parties within the world) will know and it will embarrass them.

Again, it parallels our own goals: I will be more successful in meeting my weight-loss target if I tell other people. If I keep it to myself, I can wriggle out but if I tell others, they will hold me accountable. It is just the same when striking a deal with someone else.

The bigger the announcement, the greater the commitment, the less the wriggle-room. Call it some grand title, give it pomp and ceremony. In their earliest known forms, diplomatic agreements were made with invitations to the gods to bear witness and any reneging, therefore, would trigger divine retribution. Such rituals are less common these days but invoking public disapproval has similar effect.

Moreover, any physical, public act towards its implementation will also increase their commitment to it. This is another of Cialdini's six rules of influencing. We have a compelling desire to be consistent with what we have already done.

In one study he cites, residents of a Californian suburb were shown a photograph of a nice house, similar to their own, with a large billboard in the front garden, obscuring the view, saying with bad lettering "Drive carefully". Not surprisingly, only 17% of those asked agreed to have such a billboard on their lawn.

In an identical suburb, another group of residents were shown the same picture and asked the same question only this time the take up rate was 76%, *five times greater*. What was the difference? The only difference was that the second group had also been asked a week beforehand to display a three inch sticker on their window saying "Be a safe driver", an insignificant request refused by no-one. This made all the difference: when asked about the billboard, they were much more likely to act consistently with this earlier, smaller deed.

These studies show that a small, low-cost but public deed significantly increases the level of commitment to the idea.

Increase their ownership of the deal

Of course, *any* act towards it, public or not, increases the likelihood they will deliver. So make them work for it. The more effort they invest in it, the less likely they will break their promise.

Anything that increases their identification with the deal or their ownership of it will increase their commitment to making it work. So let the solution be their idea. If it is their idea, they are hardly likely to think it is a bad one.

Alternatively, if you are suggesting solutions, make more than one offer at the same time. Offer different packages (each of which you are happy with) then let them choose. You will look generous and creative and they will not want to look too unco-operative by turning them *all* down. Even if they do, they are more likely to return with a modification of one of your suggestions than reject them outright. Importantly, allowing them to choose gives them ownership of the final deal and so they are more likely to implement it. Of course, there is no reason why you cannot give a choice and recommend one particular option (and, indeed, people often like having this guidance).

Get lock-in

The aim is to design your deal so that, once signed, the other party is locked into its implementation.

Some processes lock trust inherently into the deal. Consider the "I cut, you choose" method. Tweedledum and Tweedledee dividing a cake in two will not trust each other to share it equally. But should Tweedledum cut it and Tweedledee choose the portion, it is in Tweedledum's interests to divide it as fairly as possible. A real-life example of this is when two parties co-own an asset and one decides to get out. A fair method is for the first party to set the price and the other decides whether they want to buy or sell their share at this price. The motivation is therefore to name a fair price.

Len Fisher, a game theorist, suggests another method: to invoke a third option which nobody wants. In his book, "Rock, Paper, Scissors", he describes playing a 3-way version of the children's game with his daughter-in-law and grandson. The grandson proudly boasts "I *always* play rock" (Fisher suggests not dissimilar to Bart Simpson who says "Good ol' rock, nothing beats that!", which of course, Lisa uses to predict his move!). Now, with this information, the best strategy for Fisher and his daughter-in-law is to collude and for each to play paper. Any attempt to win outright by playing scissors will be beaten by the rock.

We see this in coalition governments where two parties form an agreement, and the force that binds the agreement is the threat of a third (mutually-disliked) party gaining power. Or in divorce settlements where ex-partners are forced to agree amicably because the alternative is throwing their money away in legal fees.

Of course, much as we wish to lock people in, there is a never a lock that cannot be picked so our aim is do whatever we can to maximise confidence in the deal. We have seen psychological lock-in is powerful. Build a strong relationship and a history of trust and teamwork. Do favours so they owe you. Build the relationship into a web of connected parties and interests; the more inter-linked, the harder to break out.

More concrete methods include structuring the deal so they are incentivised to deliver: payment in instalments or on delivery, increasing benefits as the agreement continues, increasing benefits as their delivery improves. Make sure your action *comes after* theirs and structure it in small steps, each of your actions contingent on them completing an action. This way you limit your exposure should they renege.

Conversely, the deal structure can also include penalty charges, high switching costs or other clauses that are sufficiently painful to deter but sufficiently plausible that it will be invoked.

It is carrot and stick: wisdom of the millennia, a cornerstone of common sense. But unfortunately common sense is not that common so let us look at it more deeply.

 Action points

Closing the deal is important but the implementation is most important of all.

▸ Flush out any potential disagreements before you close the talks

▸ Anticipate future scenarios and include a dispute settlement procedure

▸ Get all of this in writing

▸ And get lock-in through penalty clauses, by using the pressure of public commitments or other methods.

Does it ever pay to cheat?

Let us examine the starkest case – downright cheating. Does it ever pay to cheat? If it does, you may decide "Forget win-win, Simon, I'm out of here, I'm going to cheat. All's fair in love and war and negotiation."

Now, before you close the book and rush out the door wearing your best cheating suit, bear in mind that if it is a better strategy for you to cheat then it is a better strategy for *everyone else* to do so too. Ok, you counter, half-way through the door, if everyone else is cheating, you should *definitely* cheat. To quote the epigraph to Joseph Heller's Catch-22:

"From now on, I'm thinking only of me"

Major Danby replied indulgently with a superior smile: "But, Yossarian, suppose everyone felt that way."

"Then," said Yossarian, "I'd certainly be a damned fool to feel any other way, wouldn't I?"

Makes sense to Yossarian but, unfortunately, as a universal strategy, it spirals down into anarchy and we all end up worse off. Not good.

What to do?

This is an important question because, ethics apart, maybe there are times when it is in your best interests not to collaborate. Maybe there are times when your counterparty should not collaborate and this will impact how much you can trust them and therefore your negotiation strategy.

Real life is complicated, eh?

Are people good or are people evil? Can you trust people? Should you be good, should you be selfish, should you be manipulative, should you be a mixture? I asked my mum these questions when I was a kid – she mumbled something vague then said she had to do the laundry.

It is difficult to resolve these questions in real life with any degree of scientific certainty because it is so difficult to isolate causes and to measure effects. The answers will depend on your experience, on your culture, on your mood of the day, on their mood of the day.

In 1980, Professor Robert Axelrod, a game theorist, tried to cut through these complications by using a more controlled virtual environment. He ran a competition where entrants submitted computer programmes to win a Prisoner's Dilemma tournament. The Prisoner's Dilemma is a mainstay of game theory, and represents a situation where participants can either co-operate or cheat. As in Catch-22, the individual's best strategy is to cheat; however, this is true for both participants in the game and should both participants cheat, everyone is worse off. Each individual choosing their own optimum solution results in all parties worse off.

Each programme represented a different strategy (for example, "always co-operate" or "randomly cheat or co-operate") and the tournament was designed to see which was the most effective when pitted against a world of other strategies.

Its format broke the collaborate/compete dilemma down to its simplest measurable elements and then, from the wide range of strategies submitted, played each one against the other repeatedly over a very large number of times.

It turned out that the simplest strategy of them all was the most successful.

The winner, 'Tit-For-Tat', as designed by Anatol Rapoport, said "Start by co-operating and then copy what the other party does from then on". In other words, if they play tough, you play tough; if they co-operate, you co-operate.

Tit-for-tat, carrot and stick, an eye for an eye: wisdom of the millennia. It seems ironic that it took some of the greatest minds of the 20th century and huge amounts of computing power to discover it again. What next? The wheel?

Maybe life is not so complicated after all.

Why was 'all quiet' on the Western Front?

An astonishing example of the Tit-For-Tat strategy evolved in the trench warfare of World War 1 between the German and Allied troops. According to studies by Tony Ashworth and described by Axelrod, troops on both sides tried, remarkably, to avoid firing at each other. If the English fired a fusillade and killed 5 Germans, the Germans would fire back until they had killed 5 Englishmen. If the French fired a shot over the trenches, the Germans would

---

Simon Horton

fire two shots back. But neither side would *intentionally* fire the first shot.

It was a tactic that evolved early on, even in 1914 there were 'truces' at mealtimes, at bad weather breaks and, famously, at Christmas when they played a game of football in No-Man's Land between the trenches. And slowly these truces would extend. People would notice that neither side deliberately defected first. But that if, for whatever reason, one side did defect there would be immediate retaliation.

For the squaddie in the trenches, of course, this was by the far best tactic. No-one got hurt! But for the top brass back at HQ, trying to win a war, it was not so good. So the troops would have to occasionally fire to show they were being serious! But, even then, they would deliberately miss. Snipers would fire repeatedly and successfully at the same spot to show how accurate they could be, and how destructive, if they wanted.

The artillery would build a pattern so predictable that the opposing colonel could walk towards the spot being shelled, safe in the knowledge it would stop by the time he got there.

This was to show to their superior officers that they were being belligerent and trying to win the war but, at the same time, showing to their counterparty they could be trusted with a deal.

But if either side did break the deal, there would be immediate angry retaliation.

Tit-For-Tat on the battlefield.

When will I see you again?

Of course, Tit-For-Tat relies on there being further meetings between the two parties or, at least, a sufficiently large chance that the parties will meet again. Otherwise there will be no opportunity for the Tat to be countered with a Tit. Under such circumstances, a scoundrel or rapscallion may be tempted to play a dastardly game knowing there is no threat of retribution.

A repeat player is someone who regularly engages in a particular type of negotiation, a one-off player is someone for whom this may be their only time. If you are buying a car from a dealer, for example, you may be a one-off player, they will be a repeat player. Clearly, repeat players have greater knowledge and skills than the one–off.

Repeat players working with other repeat players know that if they do not act in good faith it will undermine any future deals and they will lose out in the long-term. However, when a repeat player is up against a one-off, they may be tempted (often encouraged) to take advantage of this power difference, *knowing that they are unlikely to meet that one-off player again.*

Remember Michael Lewis's description of the bond trader who constantly asks, "How cunning is my opponent? Does he have any idea what he's doing, and if not, how do I exploit his ignorance?".

Disreputable bond traders actively looked for the fool in the game and the fool was invariably the person who did not know the rules, the outsider, the person who is not a repeat player.

It is not just bond-traders. Car dealers, financial salespeople, estate agents, lawyers and any other repeat player taking advantage of trusting and unsuspecting members of the general public who do not know the rules.

If you find yourself as a one-off negotiating with a repeat player, get back-up. Draft in expertise from someone who *is* a repeat player. Don't be a fool.

Don't put your neck under their foot

Repeat players are likely to come across their counterparties again so need to be wary of retribution. But it does not even need to be that individual. You may build a reputation in your field or neighbourhood that will precede you and will cause difficulties in the future.

In a way, we never deal with a one-off situation. You may not meet them but you meet their bigger brother. Or their angry son. Or a friend of theirs who was once told a story about an untrustworthy individual who...

It is a remarkably small world and there is a very high chance that what goes around will come around at some point. To quote Leigh Steinberg, the top American sports agent on whom Tom Cruise's character Jerry Maguire was modelled: "The one sure thing that I know about business is that, if you've got your foot on someone else's neck, at some point in the future, that person will have his foot on your neck."

Imagine: your neck is under their foot, how do you want them to behave? Well think about that the next time you find yourself with your foot on theirs. Act magnanimously. Just because you have the power does not mean you have to use it. Consider it an insurance premium.

 Action points

Use Tit-for-Tat:

▸ Be nice: start by co-operating and continue as long as they do

▸ Be provocable: retaliate as soon as they defect

▸ Forgive: co-operate again when they resume co-operation

▸ Be clear: let them know what you are doing, and why, so they know what to expect

▸ Do not be envious: maximise your return, forget about theirs

▸ Use Tit-for-Tat + 1 – let them off the first instance but be very clear about your next response

▸ Be extra cautious if they are a repeat player and you are not; be extra cautious if you are only likely to deal with them this once.

9.4 WHAT TO DO IF YOU REALLY CAN NOT TRUST THEM AT ALL

And, finally, what if you are negotiating with someone who you absolutely know you cannot trust?

Joel Brand and Rudolf Kasztner were two Hungarian Jews who found themselves negotiating with Adolf Eichmann, the Nazi SS colonel in charge of the Final Solution, the murder of all Jews in German territories.

This was 1944 and the Germans were in total military control of the region and knowledge of the millions already deported and murdered was widespread. Why would you negotiate with such a monster? Answer: utter desperation. A tougher question: *how* do you negotiate with such a monster? How could you trust a single word he said?

Working from the premise that even a single life is worth saving if there is a way, Kasztner and Brand looked for any potential grounds for a deal. They thought the Germans may be open to bribery in return for saving the lives of Hungarian Jews.

There were a couple of problems. Firstly, they had no money. Secondly, even if they had, the Germans could just take it anyway, such was their power in the circumstances. Since taking control in Budapest, they had established a very efficient, systematic programme to rob the Jews of all their wealth. They had no need to offer any concession in return.

But "the Germans" or "the SS" were not one person. And in the detail there was a chance. Maybe *individual* Germans wished to enrich themselves personally and here was the opportunity. Moreover, the money they promised was *extra* money, money from outside of Hungary, from contacts in Turkey and Palestine.

So they targeted Captain Dieter Wisliceny, an SS-Hauptsturmfuhrer, and offered $2m. Wisliceny agreed to see what he could do but said that $2m would not be enough and, over time, more money would be required.

Perhaps they had found leverage, after all. But they were not fools, there was absolutely no trust. So they raised a first instalment of $200,000 from within the Budapest Jewish community and demanded to see something positive in return. Their sources, they claimed, were not willing to produce any further payment until they saw a result.

And this worked. Wisliceny asked them for a list of the first group of 600 people that would be sent to safety in Palestine.

But, of course, it did not work. When you negotiate with evil people and you have no power, do not expect things to go smoothly. Kasztner soon heard that, counter to their agreement, all Jews were to be ghettoised and then deported. And now Wisliceny was nowhere to be found. That down-payment of $200,000 was lost with nothing to show for it.

But the negotiations took a twist. Adolf Eichmann summoned first Brand then Kasztner to talk. As it turned out, there was something that the Jews could give him and he was someone who had authority to deliver.

He told them he was willing to spare one million Jews in return for the provision of 10,000 trucks, required for the war-effort. He thought rich Jews in the world outside the Axis territories would be happy to provide them and, to make it easier for them to agree, he promised they would only be used on the Eastern Front. Fighting Soviet Russia, he thought, was something that would not concern Great Britain and the United States too much.

But how much is the devil's promise really worth?

They were quite sure Eichmann would spare no-one and, indeed, even as they were talking the deportations accelerated. Eichmann, for his part, did not believe they could deliver either – he did not believe it was within their power. And, sure enough, Brand was arrested but the British in Syria trying to organise the truck delivery and was detained for the rest of the war. But the outcomes were so important to both sides that Eichmann and Kasztner kept the talks alive, playing for time, hoping that something would arise.

Eventually, a train was prepared, destination Switzerland, and Kasztner even negotiated a higher number to be saved, increasing his list from 600 people to a total of 1684 who boarded.

But remember, this was dealing with the devil. The train did not go Switzerland. It went to Belsen, the infamous concentration camp.

The negotiations continued. Kasztner opened talks with another SS colonel, Kurt Becher. Becher was a political rival to Eichmann and had different objectives. By now, Germany was sure it was going to lose the war and Becher was more concerned about the aftermath. Kasztner promised he would inform the allies of any help Becher provided in saving Jews.

With Becher's help, finally, six months after leaving Budapest, the train was allowed to move from Belsen and arrived safely in Switzerland. Becher and Kasztner continued to travel around other concentration camps, negotiating the peaceful handover of the camps to the Allies, thereby saving Jewish lives in direct contradiction to Hitler's explicit orders to kill all inmates before handover.

Brand and Kasztner's intentions have been debated amongst certain circles since the war, along with the extent of their impact. But there can be no doubt that they managed to get some result (and if they only saved one life, that alone is massive) in a situation where they had absolutely no power and they were negotiating with people who could not be trusted at all.

Psychopaths amongst us?

Psychologists identify a dark triad of personality traits – narcissism (egotistical vanity), machiavellianism (manipulative behaviour) and psychopathy (amoral behaviour combined with very low empathy). Their commonality is lack of empathy for another person. In the eyes of such people, the other person only exists to serve them.

With such people, you need a different negotiation strategy!

According to Babiak and Hare, most studies on such personalities, especially psychopaths, have been conducted on prison-inmates. It is now beginning to be understood, though, that they are more common in society at large than we think and often show a very normal face to others. They suggest a figure of 1% of the population at large, other studies suggest as high as 4%. That means one in 25 people, so you will meet them. And they do not wear psychopath hats, they are often difficult to identify. They are often very good at adopting an acceptable persona, like Bernie Madoff, a pillar of the highest society who managed to "lose" $65bn from his clients' accounts, many of whom were his closest and oldest friends.

It does not mean that you cannot get through to these people. As we saw with Eichmann, even a psychopath can be influenced if you put your message in terms of benefit for them. Furthermore, it is very rare that an individual is *totally* devoid of empathy for the other. Leonard Wolf (the father of Naomi Wolf and, in his own right, author and renowned horror expert) interviewed a ten-times serial killer who said "I had to turn that (empathic) part of me off", which implies even such an extreme case still has the ability to empathise and your aim is to reach that.

What else can you do if you find yourself at the negotiation table with someone who shows psychopathic tendencies?

How to negotiate with crocodiles

As the song says, "Never smile at a crocodile". Well, you can but if it smiles back, worry.

Most people, faced with a croc, would get as far away as possible as quickly as possible. That is the sensible strategy. But if you find yourself in a position where you are obliged to deal with one, you certainly would not rely on its altruism to reach a win-win. Crocodiles eat their own young, for goodness sake.

So let us say you are a zoo-keeper and you want to move a particular croc from one cage to another and you do not want to resort to the "nuclear" option of tranquilising it. You would probably:

- Consider whether you really have to do this or not
- Ask is there someone better qualified than you available?
- Make sure you are well-trained
- Make sure you have a lot of support
- Make sure you have the nuclear option (a tranquiliser or even a live bullet) as a back-up
- Reduce its capability of hurting you (eg, by a noose around the jaws)
- Tempt it with a trail of meat that will take it where you want it to go
- You may give it a push in the right direction as a start
- Reduce its options of going elsewhere by blocking off escape routes.

Similar principles apply if you find yourself negotiating with a human "crocodile"!

Meanwhile, back on planet earth...

I do not want you to go running away with the idea that everyone out there is a psychopath and no one can be trusted. Far from it. And even a psychopath does not murder everyone he meets! I have met several thousand people in my life and at 1% that would include many psychopaths. I have never been serially killed by anyone yet.

We are simply considering worst-case scenarios.

Remember: the Strong Win-Win approach says trust appropriately. This means look to trust because there is a trust dividend to be claimed.

Assume that mostly you can trust. But know how to tell if you cannot trust someone and know what to do if you really cannot trust them at all.

This approach will bring success in most instances but not all. Strong Win-Win does not work if the earth is struck by a meteorite, if there is a nuclear explosion in your vicinity, or if you are dealing with a psychopath backed by a large army. Fortunately, all of these scenarios *are extremely unlikely*.

In all other cases, follow the Strong Win-Win approach and you will get your result. Even if that result means going elsewhere for your Plan B.

But in case this talk has upset you, here is a story that shows there is always hope of a happy ending, even with psychopaths and crocodiles. Feel free to listen to the "Love Theme from Romeo and Juliet" as you read the next section.

Never smile at a crocodile, well...

That Jungle Book song has some pretty good advice. But it is not advice that Gilberto Shedden follows.

Shedden, also known as Chito, is a 52 year old Costa Rican farmer who came across a 17ft crocodile in the jungle. The croc was injured, he had been shot in the head and left to die. An injured giant croc with a hatred for humans normally spells "R-U-N"! But Chito thinks differently to most human beings.

He loaded the croc on to his boat and took it to his farm where he treated its wound and gave it medicine and food. He gave it a name, Pocho, took it into his house to care for it and he would even sleep next to it at night. "I just wanted him to feel that somebody loved him, that not all humans are bad". No, but

---

maybe some are crazy! Eventually Pocho got better and, of course, had to be returned to the wild. They loaded him back on to the boat and took him to a lake where they let him into the water and Chito said his goodbyes.

But, like all the best love stories, it was not over yet.

Remarkably, the crocodile climbed out of the water and followed Chito home! It was love!

The relationship blossomed. 20 years after they first met, they are still best friends. Pocho comes when Chito calls his name. They will swim together and roll around in the water. Chito hugs him, rides on his back, rolls him over, even kisses him on his nose.

It is reckoned that Pocho is about 50 years old. So the two of them are pretty much the same age, they are from the same neighbourhood, they have got a lot in common – man, its the power of rapport!

20 years on, still best friends. And all the time that crocodile is smiling...and so is Chito.

(as reported in the Daily Mail, 17 Aug 2009)

AFTERWORD

There you have it. Everything you need to become a master negotiator.

Now, get out there and put it into practice. Everything in this book is theory, it only becomes real when you do something with it. Remember, no one ever learnt to swim by reading a book.

And as you put it into practice, I urge you to do so ethically. Ethics are really outside the domain of this book. I would like the world to be a better place and much of my work is conducted with that in mind but I am not writing the new Sermon on the Mount. I will leave it to the philosophers and the clergymen to discuss such matters and I will leave it to you to make your own moral choices.

But, that said, let me ask you a question: what are you voting for? Are you voting for war, gangs and fear on the streets? Or are you voting for greater wealth for everyone, in both monetary and non-monetary terms. Your actions are your votes. Whatever you may say at dinner parties or shouting at the television, it is your actions that count. If you act deceitfully or play hard-ball, you are voting for a world of deceit and conflict and you may well get it. And you will not be able to complain the next time you hear of a Madoff scandal or a politician decides to build a road in your backyard or a kid steals your wallet. It is the world you voted for.

Roger Fisher once told John Grinder the story of a plane hurtling to the ground and the captain says to the co-pilot, "You need to pull your socks up or you're going to be in trouble". We *all* need to pull our socks up or we are *all* in trouble. It is no good pointing our fingers at others – at the banks, at the regulators, at the press, at the politicians, at the unemployed, at the super-wealthy – it is all of us. We are all in it together and we all need to change.

Your actions (yes, mine too) contribute to your culture so create the culture you want to see. Have you ever noticed when queuing in a supermarket, that if you are friendly and chatty to the checkout-attendant, they will in turn be much friendlier to the next person in the queue? It creates a ripple effect. And it creates a greater chance that the next time you are there, the person *in front of you* will be friendly and chatty to the checkout–attendant, so they will then be automatically nice and friendly to you.

If this does not persuade you, that is fine, I have an ace up my sleeve. In fact, forget the ace, this is my Smith & Wesson. The most compelling reason to be ethical in your dealings is that it actually gets you your best deal. The reason being that the win-win approach to negotiations creates extra value in the deal, you spend more time creating and less time fighting. Your share of that greater value is more than if you won through a win-lose approach. What is more, you can be assured that the deal will be implemented as agreed.

So be good, like your mamma said, and you will get your best deal. For purely selfish reasons, the win-win approach is best.

And win-win is infectious. When people see the positive gains it brings, they catch on and do it more. If you arm-wrestle, even if you win, it is exhausting. Win-win is easier, quicker, less tiring, more fun and the win is bigger. It is a no-brainer.

Of course, win-lose arm-wrestlers are still around. Which is why we have introduced the Strong Win-Win system. Use that and you can be confident in leading the way to win-win. Even the arm-wrestler can be persuaded to go win-win and as they do, they see the benefits, so they will try to do it themselves in the next negotiation. It is another ripple effect slowly progressing through the world.

And one last thing, one last little technique for becoming a negotiation master: be in touch with your vision. There is an apocryphal story of three people working on a building site and one of them is asked what he is doing, he replies he is laying bricks. The second is asked what the same question and replies he is building a church. The third is asked and replies, "I am building a house for God". Now, whatever your religious views may be, it is easy to see that this third person will be the most motivated and the most energised in their work, they will lay the bricks most expertly, they will love their work the most and will be most dedicated to becoming a master.

You will be inspired to master negotiation by a vision bigger than the negotiation itself. So what is your vision? What inspires you? Is it to make lots of money? Fine. Is it the joy of negotiating in itself? Or to become the great negotiating superhero making the world a better place (wearing a lycra suit and your underpants on the outside)? Whatever is your vision, get back in touch with it.

Now, you have probably all seen someone who is such a good negotiator, they just seem to create results out of magic. Well, it was not magic, they had a technology.

You, too, now have that technology. With the tools you have read in the preceding chapters, go out and perform magic. Surprise, astonish, inspire. To get the best deal you can, to build the best life you can and, yeah, why not, to build the best world you can.

The Alternative Contents Page

Further reading

Roger Fisher & William Ury, "Getting To Yes", Fisher & Ury

William Ury , "Getting Past No: Negotiating with difficult people", Century Business (1991)

Roger Fisher & Daniel Shapiro, "Beyond Reason: Using emotions as you negotiate", Random House (2005)

David Lax & James Sebenius, "3-D Negotiation: Powerful tools to change the game in your most important deals", Harvard Business School Press (2006)

Robert Mnookin, "Bargaining with the Devil: When to negotiate, when to fight", Simon & Schuster (2010)

Zartman And Berman, "The Practical Negotiator", Yale University Press (1983)

Max H. Bazerman & Margaret A. Neale, "Negotiating Rationally", Simon & Schuster (1993)

Roy J. Lewicki, David M. Saunders, John W. Minton, Bruce Barry, "Negotiation: Readings, exercises and cases. 4th Edition" McGraw Hill (2003)

G.R. Berridge, "Diplomacy: Theory and practice", Palgrave (2010)

Raymond Cohen, "Negotiating Across Cultures: International communication in an interdependent world", United Institute of Peace Press (1997)

Rasmus Tenbergen, "Principled Negotiation and the Negotiator's Dilemma – is the "Getting to Yes" approach too "soft"?", Paper presented at the Interdisciplinary Research Seminar on Negotiation, Harvard University, May 2001

Barry & Friedman, "Bargainer Characteristics in Distributive and Integrative Negotiation", Journal of Personality and Social Psychology, Vol 74, No 2, pp 345-359, 1998

Fredrik Stanton, "Great Negotiations: Agreements that changed the modern world", Westholme Publishing (2010)

Gary Noesner, "Stalling for Time: My life as an FBI hostage negotiator", Random House (2010)

George J. Mitchell, "Making Peace: The behind-the-scenes story of the negotiations that culminated in the signing of the Northern Ireland Peace Accord told by the American Senator who served as independent chairman of the talks", University of California Press (1999)

May & Zelikow, "The Kennedy Tapes: Inside the White House during the Cuban Missile Crisis", W.W.Norton (2002)

Jimmy Carter, "Talking Peace: A vision for the next generation", Puffin (1995)

George Herring, "The Pentagon Papers", McGraw Hill (1993)

Ricardo Semler, "Maverick: The success story behind the world's most unusual workplace", Arrow Books (1993)

Michael Lewis, "Liar's Poker: The book that revealed the truth about London and Wall Street", Hodder & Stoughton (1989)

John Man, "The Leadership Secrets of Genghis Khan", Transworld Publishers (2009)

Robert Greene, "The 48 Laws of Power", Viking Press (1998)

Crocodile crazy: The man who enjoys giving his dangerous 'companion' kisses and cuddles
http://www.dailymail.co.uk/news/article-1206872/Crocodile-crazy-The-man-enjoys-giving-dangerous-companion-cuddle.html#ixzz1rdt9kJ4o

Erik Qualman, "Socialnomics: How social media transforms the way we live and do business", Wiley (2010)

Richard Branson, "Business Stripped Bare: Adventures of a global entrepreneur", Virgin Books (2010)

James Wallace & Jim Erickson, "Hard Drive: Bill Gates And the making of the Microsoft empire", Harper Paperbacks (1993)

Frank Abagnale and Stan Redding, "Catch Me If You Can: The true story of a real fake", Mainstream Publishing (2003)

http://www.guardian.co.uk/film/2010/nov/11/dick-van-dyke-porpoises-rescue

Robert B. Cialdini, "Influence: The psychology of persuasion", Quill (1984)

Karen Pryor, "Don't Shoot the Dog", Ringpress (2002)

Robert Dilts, "Strategies of Genius, Vol 1", Meta Publications (2005)

Varieties of Double Bind Erickson & Rossi, The American Journal of Clinical Hypnosis, January 1975. Reprinted in Collected Papers Volume 3.

Shultz Von Thun, "Miteinander Reden Kommunikationspsychologie für Führungskräfte", Rowohlt Tb (2003)

Http://News.Bbc.Co.Uk/1/Hi/Uk/8660688.Stm - Iranian Embassy Hostage Negotiations, Chinese Whispers

Timothy Gallwey, "The Inner Game of Tennis", Pan (1986)

French and Raven, "The Bases Of Social Power" in Cartwright and Zander, "Group Dynamics", New York: Harper & Row, 1959.

Fast Company Magazine, "The Wal-Mart You Don't Know", Charles Fishman, December 1, 2003

Greenpeace Annual Report 2009/Cargill 2010 Summary Annual Report/Nestlé 2009 Financial Report

http://www.people.hbs.edu/acuddy/in%20press,%20carney,%20cuddy, %20%26%20yap,%20psych%20science.pdf

Rosenthal & Jacobson, "Pygmalion in the Classroom", Holt Reinhart and Winston (1968)

Tazelaar, Van Lange & Ouwerkerk, "How to overcome the detrimental effects of noise in social interaction: The benefits of generosity", Journal of Personality and Social Psychology, Vol 82(5), May 2002, 768-780.

Jones, Pelham, Carvallo & Mirenberg, "How Do I Love Thee? Let Me Count the Js: Implicit Egotism and Interpersonal Attraction", Journal of Personality and Social Psychology, 2004, Vol. 87, No. 5, 665–683

Dan Ariely, "Predictably Irrational: The hidden forces that shape our decisions", Harper (2008)

Stuart Sutherland, "Irrationality", Pinter and Martin (1992)

Daniel Kahneman, "Thinking Fast, Thinking Slow", Allen Lane (2011)

Jason Zweig, "Your Money and Your Brain: Become a smarter, more successful investor the neuroscience way", Souvenir Press (2007)

Michael McMaster & John Grinder, "Precision: A new approach to communication. How to get the information you need to get results", Grinder, Delozier and Associates (1993)

Donatella Meadows, "Thinking in Systems: A primer", Earthscan (2009)

Paul Babiak & Robert Hare, "Snakes in Suits: When psychopaths go to work", Harper (2006)

Sharon Jakobwitz & Vincent Egan, "The Dark Triad And Normal Personality Traits", Personality And Individual Differences 40 (2006) 331–339

"Disordered Personalities At Work" Authors: Belinda Jane Board; Katarina Fritzon , Psychology, Crime & Law, Volume 11, Issue 1 March 2005 , Pages 17 - 32

Francis Fukuyama, "Trust: The social virtues and the creation of prosperity", Simon & Schuster (1995)

Stephen M.R. Covey, "The Speed of Trust: The one thing that changes everything", Simon & Schuster (2006)

Watson Wyatt, "Work USA 2002", http://www.watsonwyatt.com/research/printable.asp?id=w-557

Robert Wright, "Non-Zero: History, evolution and human co-operation", Little Brown (2000)

Robert Axelrod, "The Evolution of Co-operation", Penguin, 1984

Michael Grinder, "The Elusive Obvious: The science on non-verbal communication", Michael Grinder & Associates (2007)

Aldert Vrij, "Detecting Lies And Deceit: Pitfalls And opportunities", Wiley (2008)

Allan & Barbara Pease, "The Definitive Book of Body Language", Orion (2004)

Paul Ekman, "Telling Lies: Clues to deceit in the marketplace, politics and marriage", W.W. Norton (1985)

Paul Ekman, "Emotions Revealed: Understanding Faces and Feelings", Phoenix (2003)

Joe Navarro with Marvin Karlins, "What Everybody is Saying: An ex-FBI agent's guide to speed reading people", Collins Living (2008)

Depaulo, Lindsay, Malone, Muhlenbruck, Charlton & Cooper, "Cues To Deception. Psychological Bulletin, 129, 74-118 (2003)

Larcker & Zakolyukina, "Detecting Deceptive Discussions In Conference Calls", Rock Center For Corporate Governance Working Paper Series No. 83

Thomas Schelling, "The Strategy Of Conflict", Harvard University Press (1990)

Thomas Schelling, "Micro-Motives And Macro-Behaviour", W.W.Norton (2006)

Von Neumann And Morgenstern, "Theory Of Games And Economic Behaviour", Princeton University Press (1970)

Len Fisher, "Rock, Paper, Scissors: Game theory in everyday life", Basic Books (2008)

Douglas and Graham Walker, "The Official Rock-Paper-Scissors Strategy Guide", Simon & Schuster, 2004

Avinash K. Dixit & Barry J. Nalebuff, "The Art of Strategy: A game theorist's guide to success in business and life", W.W. Norton (2008)

Steven J. Abrams & Alan D. Taylor, "The Win-Win Solution: Guaranteeing fair shares to everybody", W.W. Norton (1999)

Steven J. Abrams & Alan D. Taylor, "Fair Division: From cake-cutting to dispute resolution", Cambridge University Press (1996)

Christoph Engel, Dictator Games: A meta-study", http://www.coll.mpg.de/pdf_dat/2010_07online.pdf

Tony Ashworth, "Trench Warfare, 1914-1918: The live and let live system", Pan (2004)

S. Shergill, Bays, Frith & Wolpert ,"Two Eyes for an Eye: The neuroscience of force escalation", Science, 11th July 2003.

Park & Rumble, "Elements Of Reciprocity And Social Value Orientation", Personality and Social Psychology, 27(10), 1301-1309 (2001)

Like it? Want more?

Want to become a Master Negotiator?

Find out about our training courses at
www.negotiation-mastery.com

Also from MX Publishing

"I wish this book had been available when I first set up in business. Unlike similar books Rebecca's book engaged me. It is practical and a doing book rather than talking at me. I would recommend this book not only to women thinking about going solo but also those who have already set up a business". **Women In Business**

"I found this book to be an excellent read from start to finish. It has a mixture of sound business advice for the budding entrepreneur combined with very interesting excerpts from the classic piece of writing by TE Lawrence."

www.mxpublishing.co.uk

Simon Horton